Improve Your Health
—— Pro-Actively ——

Dr. Maurice A. Pisciottano
Dr. Richard F. Barrett

Regain Health and Overcome Pain Now!

Real Stories from Patients and Doctors Globally
Reveal How

Published by
Pro-Solutions
McMurray, Pennsylvania

This book is intended to give guidance and support a natural path to healing. It is meant to be thought provoking and motivate the reader to become educated, take their own journey and decide what the correct form of healing for them is. Every attempt has been made to make the content of this book accurate. However, errors may occur. The philosophy and opinions of the authors do not necessarily reflect the philosophy and opinions of other natural healers.

The authors and publisher shall not be responsible to any person or entity in regards to any damages, losses, whether real or alleged from the information contained in this book.

Improve Your Health Pro-Actively
Regain Health and Overcome Pain Now!
Real Stories from Patients and Doctors Globally Reveal How

By Dr. Maurice A. Pisciottano and Dr. Richard F. Barrett

Published by Pro-Solutions
3380 Washington Road
McMurray, Pennsylvania 15317
Phone 877-942-4284

Manufactured in the United States of America

ISBN 09705431-1-5

Dedication

This book is dedicated to the billions of people on the planet who deserve the finest in natural healing. To those who seek alternatives to medications. To those who believe their right to health should not be dictated by others. It is dedicated to the millions of people who have used alternative healing as a source for their families' good health.

It is further dedicated to the thousands of chiropractors, who over the course of one hundred plus years have laid down their hands, their souls and hearts to heal another human being. It is because of those that have come before, that suffered and tirelessly toiled for others, that we are able to stand on their shoulders and continue to build on the foundation they laid.

With heartfelt gratitude we also dedicate this book to our families who believe, understand, love and support us in our profession and our dedication to serve others. It is your continued love that allows us to do what we do best.

Especially to our respective parents; Nick and Rose Pisciottano, whose courageous decision to use chiropractic care to improve their young son's health when conventional medicine advised otherwise, altered the course of his life. Not only was he healed but inspired to become a chiropractor, to teach chiropractic and deliver chiropractic care, enriching the lives of millions. To Joe and Vlasta Barrett who overcame many adversities in life and set high standards of moral and ethical behavior. Their examples coupled with their love for all human beings sowed the seeds for their son's life in chiropractic.

Finally to Dr. Walter Vernon Pierce, Sr., for his decades of dedication to chiropractic. He taught Dr. Pisciottano not only the science of chiropractic but also the art. It was on this foundation that Dr. Pisciottano built a system and techniques, including the Pro-Adjuster, enabling the delivery of highly accurate chiropractic care and impacting the health of millions of people throughout the world!

Contributing Writer Acknowledgments

This book was greatly enhanced through the contributions made from these doctors of chiropractic and their patients throughout the U.S. and the world. Thank you all for your dedication to promoting a healthier world through chiropractic and Pro-Adjusting. (Contributing doctor's names appear in alphabetical order.)

Doctors	Patients
Dr. Steve Arculeo	Diane Ziff
Dr. Shaun R. Gifford	Susie C.
Dr. Matt Goldman	Lisa DiGorio
Dr. Laurel Gretz- Pisciottano	Maxine Bysick
	Betty Frye
Dr. Jill Howe	Stew Cohen
Dr. Rebecca Kloczkowski	Bob Kloczkowski
Dr. Kevin Laster	Randy Hamilton
Dr. James Maggio	Marjorie Curtis
Dr. Sam Nia	Donald H. Rice, III
Dr. Peter G. Phillips	Barbara Lipnos
Dr. Geno A. Pisciottano	Mike Susko
Dr. Joseph Porreca	Susan Ritsko
Dr. Michele E. Quam	Wendy Carter
Dr. Donald F. Riefer	Amanda Beck
Dr. John L. Silva	Captain Darryl Cunningham
Dr. M. Travis Sizemore	Diane F. Sivacek
Dr. Robert Smigelski	Arlene Yearn
Dr. Gary Smouse	Lauren Dickerson and Mother
Dr. Jonathan F. Stein	Patty Goodman
Dr. Jason L. Strotheide	Ina Johnson
Dr. Jerrod Wright	Eileen Silva
Dr. Masa Yamasaki	Satoko Okado
Dr. Maurice A. Pisciottano	Alice Bock
	Kathleen Fleissner
	Brenda Gamrat
	Betty J. Gilmore
	Bill Harps
	Steve Newman
	Ute Phillip
	John Shomo
	Chris Tatman
	Frank Winters
Dr. Richard F. Barrett	Ursula Hayes
	Robert Whitson

Acknowledgments

We would like to thank some special individuals who helped take this book from an idea to a product. Coordination of stories, organization of material, creation of images, computer entry, proof reading, editing, and communication with doctors are just part of the incredible effort that was put forth to create this book. We are very grateful for the tireless work to make this book a reality. Thank you, Mary Barrett, Dr. Laurel Gretz-Pisciottano, Jamie Blayney, Jeff Doyle, Jim Dudiak and Brocky Brown. Special thanks to Tom Becse, John Crunick and Lou Laskey, the Pro-Adjuster engineering and development team, without whom the Pro-Adjuster may not have been realized.

Foreword

How are you feeling right now? Do you have some aches and pains? Are you sitting at home with a health problem distracting you from enjoying your life? Or are you sitting in a doctor's office right now, waiting your turn to be diagnosed or treated?

I have no idea what your particular health challenge happens to be at the moment, or what you have tried to do to help yourself feel better. But what I do know is that chiropractic treatment can alleviate your pain and most likely help you heal whatever you are struggling with. That's the good news and the promise of chiropractic care.

But that good news gets even better.

Today there is an instrument that can help you feel better faster. It's fast, gentle, and remarkably accurate. It was created by Dr. Maurice A. Pisciottano, one of the authors of this book. The other author, Dr. Rick Barrett, introduced me to the instrument one day in his office.

Dr. Barrett is a dear friend of mine, a client, and my own personal doctor. I first went to him because of some neck pains. He helped me relieve those quickly. I then kept going to him for preventive care, and just because he's fun to visit.

One day Dr. Barrett introduced me to his instrument, the one his coauthor created. I'm open to new ideas and tools, so I let him use it on me. I was amazed. The instrument caused a gentle thumping along my spine, at the key areas it signaled Dr. Barrett were out of alignment on me. As the machine gently thumped my spine, I felt my muscles relax. I felt my shoulders come down. I felt my breathing deepen. And when I turned my neck, I could turn it further than I had done at any time that entire week!

I'm sold. I was already a believer in chiropractic care. Now I'm a believer in one of its new tools — the Pro-Adjuster instrument.

You're in for a treat. This book talks about the Pro-Adjuster instrument, chiropractic care, and about real people—people just like you—who got treatment and are now experiencing fulfilling, happy, productive lives.

Now it's your turn.

What are you going to do first after you feel better?

Make a list. You're about to do everything on it!

JOE VITALE
#1 Best-Selling Author - *Spiritual Marketing*
Publicity Advisor to a major Las Vegas Hotel
Author of way too many other books to list here

Contents

About The Authors

Dr. Maurice A. Pisciottano, CEO and founder of Pro-Solutions for Chiropractic. Graduating with honors, Dr. Pisciottano received his Doctorate Degree in 1989 from Palmer College of Chiropractic in Davenport, Iowa. He pursued extensive post-graduate advanced studies at Atagona Spinal Biomechanical Engineering Research Laboratory. He is also a member of the American Clinical Applied Spinal Biomechanical Engineering. Dr. Pisciottano has built a successful multiple office practice in Western Pennsylvania, and has helped tens of thousands of people receive chiropractic care.

As well as continuing to practice chiropractic he is a noted lecturer, author and management expert. Dr. Pisciottano is internationally known for techniques, developments and systems to improve patients' health naturally. He brings this knowledge to the profession with seminars, teleconferences, instructional videos and books. Both patients and doctors continue to benefit by his expertise and ability to deliver highly accurate, pertinent and useful information in a direct and useful fashion. Dr. Pisciottano's highly acclaimed *Pro-Peak Performance* program is a dynamic energy enhancement system used internationally. He has taught this program to thousands of businesses and organizations including fire fighters, federal judges and law enforcement agencies such as F.B.I. and C.I.A.

Knowing that poverty perpetuates ill-health, Dr. Pisciottano developed a system to help people create personal wealth, thereby eliminating the burden of health care based on insurance dependence. It is called *Personal Financial Freedom.*

Dr. Pisciottano has devoted his professional career to the development of the instrumentation and the computerization of chiropractic treatment systems. In addition to the day to day mission of bringing the population to better health through chiropractic treatment, Dr. Pisciottano has made it part of his purpose to continue to bring chiropractic, as a profession, further into the scientific arena with the advancement of the Pro-Adjuster technique. He travels the world conducting speaking engagements on the topic.

As a noted authority on chiropractic analysis and treatment protocols, Dr. Pisciottano regularly teaches continuing education courses for chiropractors nationally and also speaks regularly at Palmer College of Chiropractic in Davenport, Iowa, and at Logan College of Chiropractic in St. Louis, Missouri.

Progressive Health Care Clinic, McMurray, PA
(724) 942-4444

About The Authors

Dr. Richard F. Barrett is President of Barrett Chiropractic Clinic, P.C. He holds a Bachelor of Science degree in nutrition from Park College and received his Doctorate Degree from Cleveland Chiropractic College. While attending Cleveland Chiropractic College in Kansas City, Missouri, Dr. Barrett received the Clinic Service Award in recognition of dedicated commitment and service to patients, as well as receiving a certificate of Appreciation for Outstanding Service to Cleveland Chiropractic College. He was also recognized and Published in National Deans List for Academic Excellence. Dr. Barrett runs a busy practice in the Houston, Texas area. He has successfully treated thousands of people in the U.S., Mexico and Honduras. Since 1995 he has traveled extensively to Mexico and Honduras as part of a multidisciplinary medical mission team, providing chiropractic care to the underprivileged. Dr. Barrett is dedicated to sharing natural healing methods with the world community. To fulfill part of his purpose of empowering individuals with knowledge of chiropractic and natural healing, Dr. Barrett has written two books, *Healed by Morning; Messages from God for the 21st Century on Herbs, Natural Healing & Drugs* and *Dare to Break Through the Pain; A Guide to Eliminating Back & Neck Pain Naturally Without Drugs or Surgery!* These books are providing inspiration to people throughout the world. He has been a contributing writer to several magazine publications and newspapers. Dr. Barrett is a dynamic, inspirational speaker lecturing on a variety of healing topics. He has spoken to groups such as police and fire departments, U.S. government agencies, churches, libraries, schools, as well as large corporations like Chevron, Unocal, Williams Energy and Fluor Daniel to name but a few. Dr. Barrett has been listed on the Who's Who in Leading Professionals and Executives since 1996, was honored in 2000 as a lifetime member in Strathmore's Who's Who for Leadership and Achievement. He was also awarded recipient of the Cystic Fibrosis Foundation's, "Houston's Singular Best" Award given for professional excellence and charitable and civic contributions to the Houston area. Dr. Barrett is a Pro-Solutions Advisory Board Member.

Barrett Chiropractic Clinic, P.C.
2853 Dulles Avenue
Missouri City, TX 77459
(281) 499-4810

Introduction

Welcome! You have just taken the first step on a journey of newfound knowledge. We are very excited for you because we understand firsthand the benefits of natural healthcare. Both of us have treated tens of thousands of people safely, effectively and with great success. We would like to share our experiences with you as well as the experiences of actual patients from other doctors. We want you to gain a new perspective on natural healing and understand a new breakthrough in healthcare with advanced chiropractic technology. We will speak to you via the written word with one mind. Our intent is to move, inspire, intrigue and touch your soul. By the end of this book and possibly before, we want you to be able to make a life enhancing decision! That is our goal. We believe once you understand what we have unveiled for you, your life will never be the same. You will wish you had been told this before, you will wonder why you had not done it before now and you may even be angry that it was hidden from you.

While you are reading this book we would like to ask you a favor, and that is to pretend or imagine we are one person. That person is someone you care about. It can be whoever you want or need that to be. We are your mother, father, sister, brother, son, daughter, best friend. We are sitting with you in your living room, sharing conversation and delivering to you a gift that can absolutely and will definitely change your life forever, if you choose to open and use the gift. This book truly is for you, with you in mind. Please accept it, read it, and cherish it. You may never receive a gift as powerful as this one again. You may have purchased this book yourself, but more than likely someone who truly cares about your health, your life and your future gave it to you. One thing is certain, nothing happens by chance. Please be open to the message that is intended for you.

Yours in Health,
DR. MAURICE A. PISCIOTTANO
DR. RICHARD F. BARRETT

Health is a currency one gets to preserve like a retirement plan if accurate and timely investments are consistently made.

- Dr. Maurice A. Pisciottano

Chapter One

The Journey Begins

"Strong Lives are motivated by dynamic purposes."
                              –KENNETH HILDEBRAND

It is with great pleasure that we, Dr. Pisciottano and Dr. Barrett, as well as 22 contributing doctors and their 35 patients invite you to take a journey with us. We will be exploring a new world for you and maybe a somewhat familiar world for others. It will be definitely enlightening and worthwhile. By the end of the journey we want you to be able to look back to where you started and realize your life will never be the same again. We will be telling you those things we believe are imperative for you to know.

Our purpose is to step you through an educational process with a specific end result. You will have a thorough understanding of the subject matter and will be empowered to make the correct health care choices for yourself and your family. Many people as part of human nature believe they are knowledgeable about many topics. Many of us seem to be particularly susceptible to this tendency of being "experts" at everything. The truth of the matter is that most of us are experts at a few things and are good at, or have some knowledge of many things. Most of us have little to no understanding of a great deal of things. People rely on others who are considered knowledgeable — parents, educators, news reporters, friends and others to provide information and advice. They then take this information and try to influence others with the new knowledge acting as if they are experts on the topic, whether it is comprehended or not. This happens in every aspect of life from hobbies and sports to raising children, repairing cars, and buying electronics. We know you have this happen in your life as do we.

Sometimes we deem ourselves to be experts and we hand out advice because we have been asked. Other times advice is given to help someone because we believe we know more than they do. Many times we are the ones being advised. The point is, all of us have experienced this numerous times in our lives and we will continue to do so.

However, none of us are as good or knowledgeable about as many topics as we believe ourselves to be. It is better to go to the experts to get the truth. As a young man, Dr. Barrett enjoyed repairing most anything mechanical especially cars. He was very good at it. With advanced technology and engineering it is almost impossible to take today's newer vehicles and be the same shade tree mechanic. Specialized equipment is needed and advanced knowledge is required. The car tinkering and repair world for newer vehicles has changed. Dr. Barrett is no longer an expert in this area. He is, however, an expert in the human body and chiropractic, as is Dr. Pisciottano and other doctors of chiropractic. It is this area of expertise and knowledge that we hope you will benefit from. Use this book as a training manual to understand the truth about chiropractic and reap the benefits of your new understanding in order to change the future of your health and health care needs.

Think of a simple scale from zero to ten in order to evaluate a level of expertise. Use zero as having no understanding of the subject matter and ten being an expert or professional on the subject. Varying degrees of certainty or understanding apply from the zero to the ten. One on the scale might be slight knowledge and five may be a good understanding having some personal experience with the subject or firsthand knowledge of it. Although as Chiropractors we are tens, we may be zeroes or ones in the area of engineering, computers, entertainment, brain surgery, home repair or other topics. This holds true with you also; however you are probably a ten in some area.

As Chiropractors we treat our children from the moment they are born. We treat our entire families. We receive treatments (adjustments) from each other regularly. We partake in a regime of nutritional supplements and therapies because we understand the extraordinary health benefits of chiropractic and nutrition. Therefore, we want only the best for all of our families. We are definitely at a ten on the scale. But you may be only a five, and someone else you know is likely a zero because you and they may not have the education, the experience or the expertise on this subject in order to be a ten. All of us start out as a zero on the scale of knowledge of any given subject. We can only advance up the scale on any subject matter by improving our education.We were not born Chiropractors, but because of our personal experience and our life situations, we grew to understand more, thereby advancing up the scale and finally arriving at a ten. We became the very thing that helped us in our lives—Chiropractors. What we hope, what we want for you is that as you read this book you will progress up the scale of understanding towards a ten. You will not become a ten unless you too decide to become a Chiropractor. Perhaps, however, we can get you close enough that you understand health better, understand natural healing methods, start reaching for nutritional supplements more than medications, start receiving chiropractic care, heal more naturally and be as close to an expert as you can be.

We guarantee you will be better informed by the end of the book. If you make the decision to use chiropractic care to enhance your life (if you have not already) you will become more aware, healthier and better educated.

By reading and completing this book, you will become intimately familiar with the new technology in Chiropractic analysis and technique of the system of the Pro-Adjuster. The Pro-Adjuster is the most advanced computerized method of chiropractic treatment that exists in our profession today. You will begin to see that this type of care is different than you have ever imagined that chiropractic care would be. The Pro-Adjuster equipment is designed exactly for achieving better understanding for the public. It gives more certainty to the Chiropractor, as he or she can give an adjustment that is *exactly* what is indicated for that day. On each and every visit, a new real time analysis will be done, and you will be able to see...right there on the computer monitor, which areas are still showing a problem, as well as which areas are correcting and therefore need less or perhaps no treatment. You will be able to see as well, on each and every visit where the improvement has occurred. There is really no more guess work or wondering on the part of the Doctor or the patient as to whether there was an actual change made with that day's treatment. You will see and be able to monitor your own progress, which will save you both time and money. And you will understand perhaps for the first time why Thomas Edison said, *"The doctor of the future will give no medicine but will interest his patient in the care of the human frame, in diet, and in the cause and prevention of disease."* The future is now! Please join us by taking full advantage of this technology and reaping the benefits from the #1 natural healthcare choice on the planet. Join us "tens" who enjoy healthier, pain free lives, happier healthier drug free children, and more active and lively seniors. It is all within your reach!

I am writing this to thank you for giving me my life back. I was suffering from frequent, moderate to severe headaches. They were interfering with my work. I am a unit clerk at a nearby hospital and am constantly dealing with people on the phone, so it was not easy to be pleasant when suffering with a throbbing headache. I had tried different treatments from aspirin to relaxation, which is hard to do on the job. The severity and frequency was increasing when I decided to come to Dr. Pisciottano for treatment. It was the best decision I could have made, which was sometimes hard to do with my headaches. I met your receptionist at a Dravosburg picnic and talked and planned my initial visit, which started my return to a normal life. I have been headache-free for about 4 months now. Also, my co-workers say they are happy with the laughter and smiles instead of the frowns.

- BRENDA GAMRAT

To achieve Peak Performance and improved health visit our website at www.pro-adjuster.com or call 1-877-942-4284.

Chapter Two

Drugs versus Natural Healing

"We live in a fantasy world, a world of illusion.
The great task in life is to find reality."

-IRIS MURDOCK

Why should you invest your time, or want to read this book? Because it literally could be the one thing you do for yourself that could change, even save your life! The information within this book and the knowledge you will gain is priceless compared to the time invested. It is critical to you and your family's health that you gain a new perspective on healing. That a light is shined on key health issues, so you can begin maybe for the first time to make rational informed decisions about treating your body in the best possible way. We will discuss the pros and cons of certain health care choices. But ultimately it is up to you to make the decision to be open to new information and then take action.

First let's look at why it is critical to have vital information on the current state of health care. It boils down to some simple concepts. Though you do not know us, our goal is to keep you from becoming a statistic! Our goal is to not only improve your health but to save your life. That sounds like a very bold statement but it is absolutely true. It is hard to believe that people you don't know have your best interest at heart but there are people in the world that still believe in creating a better life for people. So why not start with the most important person — YOU!

The facts from a major U.S. study revealed that over 2 million people have toxic reactions to properly prescribed medications yearly! That's approximately half the people in a city the size of Houston, Texas! The study also says that over 106,000 people die from the same prescribed medications each year. Can you imagine everyone in a city the size of Pittsburgh, Pennsylvania dying? Now imagine the inhabitants of a city that size disappearing every year. The magnitude is unimaginable. Yet that is exactly what is happening. How about where you live? Can you imagine everyone disappearing? The study goes on to suggest that this could be the fourth leading cause of death in the U.S.! Of course, we don't have statistics on the impact to the rest of the world population. It is safe to say they are dying in record numbers also.

It is so important to understand the harsh reality of the alternative to natural healing. What mainstream medicine and the drug (pharmaceutical) companies have been advertising as the truth is causing serious effects all around us. Most people do not realize that medical drugs being utilized as they are intended are responsible for prolonged continuous sickness and even death amongst large portions of the world population. Before we can begin to explain the correct way to heal and the alternatives that can help you, a serious thought must be considered. You could become a statistic! This is no joke and we take your health very seriously. No one ever wants to believe that the negative things that happen to people will ever happen to them. Our brains and emotions sometimes fool us and create a false sense of security by allowing us to believe we are immune to the troubles that others experience. Yet if we truly analyze this and shine a critical light on this subject, the reality is that if we do the same thing as someone else, the odds are we are just as likely to have the same negative event occur. In other words, if one hundred people lined up on the shoulder of the busiest freeway and tried to run through traffic to cross to the other side, the risk is the same for each person. The likelihood of one person getting killed is as good as another getting killed. The risk of one being critically injured or having minor injuries is equal to the next person. Still, some people would believe falsely that nothing would happen to them. Of course, there might be a few people who would actually make it to the other side. This is why somebody might say, "Don't worry about running across the freeway, it is safe. I did it." We all want to believe we will be the safe one, as we do not want to confront that tragedy could happen to us. It is likely that we would be horrified and appalled that this tragedy befell us. How could it have happened, might be the question of our disbelief that it occurred to us and not someone else. Most times we do not recognize the very actions that we take that put us into harm's way. Certainly the idea of people running across a busy freeway sounds insane. In that way, it seems that believing medications and surgeries hold the answer to all health issues would be unlikely. To think that medications and surgeries are always safe would also be unlikely. To think that these approaches to health issues are always going to do more good than harm is also unlikely. You see, to our way of thinking the pharmaceutical companies, and the advertising marketers are telling us that taking their drugs is okay, like it is okay to run across the freeway. That it is perfectly safe. This is simply not true. Not all of the time. The reality is that we have grown up being brainwashed into believing that medications are the answer to all of life's difficulties, and health problems. This is considered a "medical model" of thinking. We are bombarded with drug advertising on television and in print. There are billboards standing on highways touting the greatness of certain drugs. It is impossible to be alive in the United States and not see a billboard while driving, hear an ad on the car radio, get on a bus, ride in a taxi, watch a television program or go to a movie without seeing or reading a drug advertisement. They are everywhere! These campaigns are so entrenched in our society, that most people do not see it on a conscious level. The pharmaceutical companies persuade us to believe that taking medication is as simple, easy, and safe as brushing our teeth, having a cup of coffee in the morning, and reading the paper! This is not so. Drugs are harsh and dangerous. They are chemicals that are introduced into our bodies that are not normally there. These chemicals all have side effects. Does this mean that all drugs are bad and that there isn't a need for them? No, absolutely not. There is a time, and place for them, and certainly it does not go unrecognized that many lives have been saved due to medical advancements. However, the prescription drug use in this country is staggering. These chemicals are prescribed in excess quantities and under the guise that they are needed for all people all the time through all the stages of our lives! It has become so ridiculous that even animals are being prescribed anti-depressants!! That is insane! We must begin the process of erasing the "brainwashing" and replacing this medical model of thinking with some new information. Do not believe you are not susceptible to the pharmaceutical companies' propaganda. We all have been subjected to this massive marketing; therefore, we need access to correct and valid information. We need to know that it is acceptable to investigate and use different types of healing methods.

Why do we care? Why do we want to help you? Simply put; wouldn't any decent human being help another who is in pain? Of course they would! We all reach out to others at some point in our lives whether that means helping the poor in our community, feeding the hungry, or nursing a sick friend or relative. Perhaps it is a matter of donating money to our churches or synagogues to help with missions of feeding and caring for the sick people and children of the world. It is a part of all humans to want to care for others; it is woven into the very fabric of our souls to help each other. One day researchers may just discover it encoded in our DNA.

In our practices we have seen many tragedies. Like patients whose family members were not "sold" on the ideas of natural healing and died from routine medical procedures — died from taking "safe medications," died because they did not want to go against their medical doctor's advice. They died because their insurance company would pay for the dangerous treatment protocol but not for the safe natural way. They died because they thought drugs and surgery was the fastest way to solve their problem. They died because they were too closed-minded to look at other forms of healing.

Why do we want to help you? Why do we want you to read this book, to gather new information and change the way you approach pain and healing? Because we don't want you to become a statistic! In our personal lives, even we have had family members who have chosen not to listen. Some of them have become needlessly ill and debilitated, some have died. We know that it was unnecessary and perhaps avoidable. When these tragedies hit so close to home, that human instinct to help becomes even more intense.

The statistics are scary and overwhelming, yet they grow yearly. Keep in mind as well that many side effects and adverse reactions never get reported. It is impossible to determine the true extent of the problem and the problem continues to escalate on an hour by hour basis. It is therefore safe to assume that the overall statistics that are reported are higher. Here are some highly alarming statistics that you should know.

- **120,000 people die each year due to hospital medical errors.** This is equivalent to one jumbo jet crashing every day! It's 3 times the number of people killed each year in the U.S. by motor vehicle accidents.

- **1 million people each year are injured in hospitals.**
  Source: Dr. Lucian Leape adjunct professor of health policy
  at Harvard School of Public Health

- **An aspirin a day keeps the doctor away-WRONG!** It actually increases the risks for bleeding ulcers and stroke. 1,600 children die each year from adverse reactions to prescribed aspirin. Other side effects: Anemia, confusion, dizziness, and more.
  Source: *Journal of the American Medical Association*

If you have been moved by anything thus far, if you can be open minded to different information, then you have a real chance at improving your life.

What then is the alternative to dangerous medications and surgeries? What are we proposing as the best most highly used alternative source for pain relief and health improvement? You may have guessed it — chiropractic healthcare. Chiropractic with a new and improved technology that will result in rapid improvements, safely without any reason to fear. In other words, there is now a completely safe, non-invasive technique for adjusting patients. This technique allows a person's body to be changed without the use of extreme forces or pressures to the spine. There is no pain, there are no risks, and there are no side effects. What could be better than that?

We want you to know right now that this new technology may be the secret weapon to handle your health concerns. We believe there is a solution to your problems, we believe you can benefit from this solution and the solution is well within your reach!

I started intensive treatment with the Pro-Adjuster in September and at last found relief. My headaches have become less frequent and I am sleeping for longer periods of time at night without pain. I no longer need to take 3 to 4 pain pills a day just to function! Most importantly, I am able to enjoy my family again and do more with them. I thank Dr. Pisciottano for his concerns for his patients and his confidence with my case. Thank you for a great staff and their friendly and positive attitudes.
- BETTY J. GILMORE

To achieve Peak Performance and improved health visit our website at www.pro-adjuster.com or call 1-877-942-4284.

Chapter Three

Life's Treasures

"Wonders of opportunity exist for only a brief moment in time, you have to have vision in order to spot them, and take advantage of them."
                                                                    -JOHN SCULLEY

    We want to share a story about a young boy, who was very happy, energetic and extremely active. He was always playing, enjoying sports, and other outdoor activities like swimming, camping, fishing, and hiking. Although he was very active he never had pain. That is, until he was about twelve years old. Then for no apparent reason, he was struck with severe mid back pain. The situation worsened at times. While bending down or leaning over the desk at school; he would become stuck in that position and unable to straighten at all. During these episodes of immobility, the pain would take his breath away. He felt as though a knife had been driven into his spine. As you might imagine this is not a normal situation, especially for a child. The episodic duration would vary from a mere minute to perhaps thirty at a time. Gradually the back pain became a constant daily condition but the "locking up" episodes diminished. His parents took him to medical doctors for evaluations. They could not find any problem or explain the episodic pain and immobility. His family at that time had no knowledge of chiropractic; therefore, it was not an option. As pain became a constant companion, it was measured by the degree not its presence or absence. More frustrating than the pain was the inability of the medical doctors to diagnose or treat the condition. They said it was growing pains and would go away, it didn't. As years went by he learned to cope with the pain. The episodes of immobility had stopped. However, the mid back pain was now slowly traveling towards his low back!

One summer after many years of suffering he experienced a particularly bad episode of pain. His family urged him to seek medical attention again, as it had been so many years since he had been examined as an adolescent. This time they suggested seeing an orthopedist that might be more knowledgeable than the previous doctors. Reluctantly, he conceded to appease them. Though he thoroughly believed no new information would be discovered. The young man was examined, x-rayed and was told once again, there was no answer. The doctor did not know what could be wrong. He suggested that an MRI (Magnetic Resonance Imaging) be performed to provide a possible answer. The young man refused this for several reasons. One, it was too expensive. He also felt in his heart and soul that his condition was no different than the past. Lastly, he did not want to be confined inside a small MRI unit since he was claustrophobic.

After this last attempt to seek answers from a medical physician and not being given any, he resigned himself to what he had already known. He would just have to live with it. He had watched his mom suffer with back pain that did not slow her down. She worked hard all her life at home and on the job, employed in meat rooms and deli departments of grocery stores. She lifted, cut and packaged meat. She suffered with back pain since she was a 16 year old girl. The doctors diagnosed her with a missing vertebra in her spine. They wanted to perform surgery on her back and expected her to be in a full body cast for several months. But her mother said no to that. Believing that his back problem likely had a hereditary link to his mother's the young man was resigned to the fact that he would spend his life in pain.

Finally a co-worker suggested seeing his Chiropractor. It took much persuading on the co-worker's part. In his mind a chiropractic doctor was no different than a medical doctor and would most likely not have a different answer or produce a better result. All others had failed to help him so he saw no point in spending more money for another doctor to tell him that he did not know what was wrong with him. At that time, he was as ignorant to chiropractic as many people are still today. That is to say he had no experience with chiropractic. He did not know any Chiropractors, nor did he know anyone who went to a Chiropractor other than this colleague. He could not say exactly what finally convinced him to go to a Chiropractor but he did ultimately go. That was the day that changed his life! He admits to having a negative attitude when he first walked into the Chiropractor's office, but it soon disappeared. What seemed to be a genuine caring attitude as the staff greeted and welcomed him to the office initially impressed him. The reception area was open, the staff was fully visible and they were interacting with the patients who were sitting there. In fact, even the patients seemed friendly; they spoke to one another and were smiling! This was a stark contrast from most doctors' reception rooms, where most people are unhealthy and seem grim. The doctor saw him almost immediately, and he was pleasantly surprised that he did not have to wait. The doctor explained the procedures and then he was examined and x-rayed. Another moment of negative thought occurred as he heard that the doctor wanted new x-rays. After all, he had just been x-rayed by the orthopedist. The doctor explained however, that he wanted to see a standing view of his spine in weight bearing position. The Chiropractor further explained that in the previous x-rays, he had been lying down, and that in this position, the true biomechanical relationship of the spine would be obscured. The doctor also mentioned that he would compare the two sets of x-rays. This explanation made sense, so he agreed. When the man returned he brought the other x-rays.

The doctor spent more time with him comparing the x-rays, explaining his condition and suggesting a course of treatment. Apparently, an undetected childhood disease called Schuermann's was hidden in the spine. While no outward signs were present, this condition was present in the young man's spine and caused distortion of the vertebrae. The doctor showed him what it had done to the shape and quality of his spine. The Chiropractor confirmed what the man had felt all those years: It was not in his head and it was not growing pains! It was something that he as a layman could actually see! Then his joy turned to anger. All the other doctors examined him and took x-rays of his spine. Why hadn't anyone else seen this? Of course, part of the answer is that medical doctors are not trained to look at the spine and its relationship to the nervous system.

He began his treatments and started to feel different. The doctor eased his suffering, improved his health, and changed his life. He was very impressed by several things. The doctor never rushed him and was fully willing to engage in dialogue, prompting him to ask whatever questions he liked. It is not often that you can actually spend time with a doctor in a very busy office. This doctor took the time for him. What really thrilled him was that the doctor actually uncovered the problem and revealed why he had been having pain since he was a boy! After all these years someone actually said, "I understand and here is what is wrong." Not only that, but the doctor also told him how he was going to help him and that the method of care would have nothing to do with living on medications.

He loved his chiropractic experience. One day the doctor suggested that he should consider returning to school to become a Chiropractor. The doctor felt that he would be right for chiropractic and that he would enjoy it as much as he did. From the moment the suggestion was made, it was like a surge of energy, a sense of urgency and heightened awareness that went through his mind and body. It was a feeling of great excitement and anticipation. There had never been anything that made such a quick and strong impact on him as this. He knew it was right. In fact, he felt as though he did not have a choice. This was his destiny. He made the most important decision of his life. Within nine months, he left his job, his home, his friends, and family and moved to Kansas City to become a doctor of chiropractic. That man is Dr. Rick Barrett.

On a warm summer evening in August 1972, a six-year-old boy was sitting outside a famous and highly regarded Chiropractor's office in Dravosburg, Pennsylvania. As he sat on a curb facing the office, he watched patient after patient walk into this Chiropractor's office. He sat there for hours, watching patient after patient leave that office. The boy was intimately familiar with this Chiropractor and was intimately familiar with chiropractic treatment. At only six years old he had been under this Chiropractor's care for three years, one half of his young life.

The small boy originally saw this Chiropractor at three years of age for serious health problems. This boy was having such severe digestive problems that the medical physicians were recommending a complicated surgery that might leave the boy with permanent damage. Fortunately, the boy's parents had the insight to get another opinion. An opinion that was not the accepted opinion, as this one would be coming from a Chiropractor. The famous Chiropractor was able to resolve all of these health conditions and turn on the small boy's body's ability to function. And function it did! Instead of becoming a medical statistic, the young boy was able to live the normal life that he deserved. It was on this summer evening that the small boy "Moe" decided he was going to become a Chiropractor just like his doctor.

The Chiropractor, one of the great pioneers of the chiropractic profession, was Dr. Walter Vernon Pierce, Sr. The small boy grew up to become Dr. Maurice A. Pisciottano. He continued to be treated by Dr. Pierce until Dr. Pierce's very unfortunate passing in 1993.

Dr. Pisciottano grew up knowing that chiropractic was the single best choice for health care for people on this planet. Chiropractic is a way of life for him. Dr. Pisciottano watched as time went by at the many developments in the profession and continued having the same level of interest that he had in the summer of 1972. It was this high level of interest that spurred him on to become a Chiropractor, chiropractic management consultant, author, and developer of chiropractic adjusting instruments. This high level of interest drove him to develop a safe, pain free technique that could permanently change not only the chiropractic profession, but also the public perception of chiropractic as a health art. It is because of his personal life changing experiences and Dr. Pierce's influence on him that he pursued chiropractic and developed equipment to not only aid Chiropractors in giving the best treatment, but also to allow patients to receive what they deserve, the best possible care through a highly precise, measured and reproducible adjustment.

It is because we, Dr. Pisciottano and Dr. Barrett, share a vision of a world being helped by chiropractic that we are delivering the secrets of pain relief, improved health, and increased energy. This book is meant for you. We truly believe you can experience what we have. Experience the truth of chiropractic. Understand natural healing on a whole new level. We love chiropractic and know that you have a great opportunity to benefit from it. Some of you may be like Dr. Barrett reaching for it as an adult, but others will be more fortunate. You will share it with your children and grandchildren so that they may experience, as Dr. Pisciottano has, the life long benefits that chiropractic care has to offer.

Chiropractic has helped generations of individuals for well over 100 years. Spinal adjustments have been used for thousands of years by all cultures. The discoveries of early writings and cave drawings confirm this. Although the past 100 years have been the most advanced and specific, there has always been a great element of art and individual expertise with the treating doctor. Now, 21st century science, engineering and computer technology gives us the capability through specific instrumentation and equipment to effectively deliver chiropractic care, to treat nervous system interference at a higher, more precise level. We can do this with an instrument called the Pro-Adjuster developed by Dr. Pisciottano.

Now that you have read both of our stories, you may be able to understand why we have unique perspectives on health, healing and chiropractic. Neither one of us may have become Chiropractors if it weren't for our own health conditions and forces driving us to receive chiropractic care. Dr. Pisciottano has truly been blessed to experience chiropractic from a very young age. On the other hand, Dr. Barrett's life was immensely impacted by chiropractic later in life. Our experiences on a personal level and the combined experience of treating tens of thousands of people, giving hundreds of thousands of treatments that drives us to continually strive to influence others to experience the benefits of chiropractic care. It truly is our duty to disseminate positive information that can change lives. Our paths have converged to unite us in our purposes to improve the lives of others through chiropractic. To educate the population so they can experience what we know. You will find that Chiropractors are generally unique because most have stories of health improvements at the hands of another Chiropractor. The advanced technology of the Pro-Adjuster equipment developed by Dr. Pisciottano will allow patients to experience the highest level of care with safety in a very immediate way. The doctors using the Pro-Adjuster are always searching for ways to deliver the best care to their patients. Though manual adjustments to the spine have been used safely, as we and millions of others can personally attest to, there will be those people that suffer needlessly because they have fear. That fear may keep them from receiving chiropractic care. That fear may be of someone touching their spine, it may be a fear or a dislike of hearing popping noises that joints make as gases are released during an adjustment. They may fear that their spine will be twisted. There is no longer a need for people to suffer, to avoid getting help for their spinal problems. There is no longer a need for post-surgical patients to have an unsubstantiated fear of being adjusted. The Pro-Adjuster is the one piece of equipment that safely analyzes the spine to determine if each vertebra (spinal bone) is in proper alignment. This is vitally important because misaligned vertebra can interfere with the nervous system's ability to freely transmit nerve impulses throughout your body. Once a painless analysis of the spine is complete, then an exact adjustment of the vertebra can be made. Utilizing a specific, non-invasive adjusting instrument, the vertebra is gently nudged until the Pro-Adjuster sensors indicate a change has been made. It then stops the treatment automatically. There is no guesswork on the part of the doctor or the patient. There is no uncertainty as to whether a change has been made. There is no reason to fear. The actual adjustment with the Pro-Adjuster is at times underwhelming to the patient, as it really does not feel as though much has been done.

The proof of patient satisfaction, comfort and alleviation of fears or concerns is best told by a satisfied patient. Our patients uniquely understand that there are countless people suffering as they once were. They feel as we do a sense of responsibility to change attitudes and positively impact lives by sharing their stories with others. Human beings truly want to help one another. It satisfies us to reach out and share a part of us. We have, as do all our Pro-Adjuster doctors, success stories from patients that could fill volumes of books. It would literally be impossible to share every story with you. We have selected a few special cases that throughout the course of this book will be unveiled to you. These stories will be in the patients' own words and we hope they will have a profound impact on you. Bob Whitson asked us to share this story with you:

> Over 10 years ago, I started having pain in my neck each time I turned my head in any direction and my lower back would have severe pain when I sat for extended periods of

time or while standing in one position even for a few minutes. Over the years the pain had become worse, especially in the neck. It was to the point that I could not look down to read or turn my head to either side without experiencing excruciating pain.

I have been a pharmaceutical sales representative for over 35 years and my training and experience with pharmaceuticals and presenting many types of drugs to physicians taught me to believe that the proper drug could successfully treat and sometimes help in curing most illnesses. I am currently a representative for a major pharmaceutical company marketing a popular acetaminophen product for pain relief. I believe in my product and have taken it regularly for the severe pain I experience on a daily basis. Sometimes a more powerful prescription medication was the only way I could get any relief.

I have always believed that chiropractic treatment could help me, but I was somewhat hesitant to get treatments because of some anxieties I had in regard to spinal manipulation. In the meantime, another health problem was attacking me, which was causing the neck and back pain to be more intense. I began having episodes of dizziness, vertigo and loss of hearing. The confusion of trying to keep my balance and trying to cope with the terribly distorted sounds and pressure in my ears only added to the feeling of tension in my neck and back.

The medical doctors who were treating me could only come up with one solution to my dilemma...pain relievers, which only masked the symptoms but offered no cure.

As for the vertigo, dizziness and hearing loss was concerned; I was hospitalized in November 1998, for 3 days and was placed in a telemetry unit for close observation and testing. After having complete blood testing and being assured that everything was normal, I was then hooked up to a cardiac monitor. I was also given a CT scan of the head, an echocardiogram, an electroencephalogram (EEG), a carotid artery ultrasound and a peripheral vascular exam. All the tests proved to be normal but the problems were still there and even worsened over the next several months.

In April 2000, my primary care physician referred me to an ENT clinic in Houston where over a 3-month period three ENT specialists trying to find the reasons for the vertigo and hearing loss examined me. I was given a Bithermal Caloric test and an Electronystagmography (ENG) exam. There were no significant abnormal responses except that the Bithermal Caloric test revealed right ear peresis response of 25%. The examining physician could not determine a definite cause of hearing loss nor the vertigo except that the inner ear nerves were affected but no definite reason was determined. No further treatments were offered.

As the condition worsened, in June 2000, an MRI of the brain and IAC, with and without contrast were ordered to determine if the condition was a result of possible brain origin. The results, however, came back normal except for a small polyp or retention cyst at the floor of the right maxillary sinus. This was in no way related to my symptoms.

Then in June 2001, a new primary care physician after hearing my complaints and reviewing my medical records was curious and concerned enough with my condition to order x-rays of the spine (cervical spine series). These tests revealed severe degenerative arthritis, bone spurs, osteoporosis and multi-level disc disease. This doctor felt that the bone spurs in my neck might be irritating the nerves in the spine and could be the reason for the severe neck and back pain and also the vertigo. He sent me to a leading neurologist who did another EEG, which was normal. The neurologist referred me to Baylor Center for Balance Disorders to undergo therapy, since in his opinion, this was a condition I would "just have to live with" and the therapy should help. I declined the treatment because I was more interested in getting rid of the problem rather than just 'learning to live with it.'

I did however, just live with it, until one year later when it seemed as if a miracle was beginning to happen in my life. I held on steadfastly to this promise but there was more I needed to do.

One evening in March, 2002, my wife, Marie, and I were shopping in Borders Book Store. She saw a book written by Dr. Richard Barrett, *Dare to Break through the Pain,* and brought it over to me. With excitement in her voice, she said, 'Bob, look at this book! This just may be the answer to our prayers. Dr. Barrett shows how chiropractic can help you in your situation and that you don't have to suffer the pain you are having and possibly even avoid surgery. And, Bob, he is located right here in Sugar Land!!' She further commented, 'I believe God led me to this book and this may be the answer to your healing.' My wife and I both believe that if God is speaking to us about a situation, it is always wise to act on it without hesitation. We did just that. We bought the book and started reading it that night. It was late but I did not want to put the book down. I could hardly wait till the next day when I finished reading it. It was so interesting, informative and convincingly offered me the drug-free, pain free and surgery free choices I had been seeking for almost four years that I was anxious to meet with Dr. Barrett for consultation. Instead of calling his office for an appointment, I went to his office, which was about 20 minutes away from our home and talked to Mary, the office manager. She was so kind, considerate and helpful in giving me material to read and assuring me that Dr. Barrett would explain all the details of his treatment procedures and answer any questions I had concerning chiropractic. While I was there, I saw another book which Dr. Barrett had just recently written, *Healed by Morning*. I was anxious to read this book since his first one was why I was at his office inquiring about his treatments. When I bought this book, I had no idea that in addition to the incredible healing powers that chiropractic offers that this book would also contain words of inspiration, wisdom and the assurance that each of us reading the book may also be used as instruments of healing others as evidenced by messages taught in the scriptures. When I started reading *Healed by Morning*, I read the entire book in one evening. By the time I reached chapter 14, 'A Time to Choose', I knew I had made the right decision to accept Dr. Barrett's chiropractic treatments as God's way of restoring my health.

In August 2002, I was examined by Dr. Barrett and the treatments began immediately. He was so careful and considerate of my situation and he explained in detail every move he made in the realignment of my spine. The anxieties that I had were gone after the first treatment because his techniques were so skillfully and carefully done and each was explained as he did them. He also explained to me that in order for me to regain my freedom of movement and to be free of the pain, I would need to be committed to treatments on a regular basis for several weeks, even months if necessary. I started in August getting 3 treatments each week and I started noticing some relief from pain after the first week. Soon after that, Dr. Barrett showed me a new and highly technical instrument called the Pro-Adjuster, which is used to adjust and realign the spine while sitting upright in a comfortable position.

The procedure is comfortable, pain free and eliminates the need for the traditional manipulation procedures on the table for some conditions. He assured me that because of the nature of my condition, this new, highly technical approach to treatment would be ideal for me. I was amazed to learn about the accuracy of the Pro-Adjuster in realignment of the spine and the adjuster is virtually error-proof. I could actually see on the screen what changes were taking place after the adjustment and could get a copy printed out to take home to track my improvement. This innovative treatment is fast, virtually pain free and leaves me feeling very relaxed.

It has been over 3 months now and my pain has been decreasing in frequency and intensity much faster than I expected. Now the pain in my neck occurs only 1 or 2 times in a week and is usually very low to moderate pain when it does occur.

I now need to go for treatments only 2 times per week and will soon be able to go less often than that. I do not have to take pain relievers on a regular basis and usually when pain occurs it is gone by the time I leave the doctor's office. My ability to move my head in any direction has also greatly improved.

One of the most exciting rewards of my treatments by Dr. Barrett with the Pro-Adjuster came somewhat as a surprise to me. I did not expect the reward since our focus was to treat the cause of pain. After several weeks of treatments I began to notice the debilitating agony and emotional trauma I suffered because of the vertigo problem was slowly but surely diminishing. It does not present a serious day to day problem unless I lift a lot or turn my head quickly. Even then, it is less severe.

For over 10 years I had become convinced that living with pain was a burden I would have to bear and the vertigo was a condition I would have to learn to live with the rest of my life. But, today, I am so thankful that I am being healed and will continue to be healed because it is God's will that we live a healthy life.

- BOB E. WHITSON

One of Dr. Pisciottano's patients was anxious to share this story of healing. Hoping that another person could be touched by the words and be motivated to take the necessary steps to change their health.

I became a patient at Progressive Health Care Clinics on June 27, 2000. On March 3, 1987, I was working on a car that was hooked to the back of a tow truck. The front end of the car was being held in the air by hooks and I was standing under the car. The car came off the hooks and crushed me beneath it. As a result, I had a compound fracture of my left ankle, a crushed right knee, L4-L5 disc blow-out, lower neck disc blow out and injuries to my internal organs.

I have since had surgery on my lower back to fuse my L3, L4 and L5 region. Titanium rods have been surgically implanted in my back and then taken out. My C6 and C7 vertebra have also been fused. On December 24, 1998, I suffered a stroke. From that time forward, I have endured constant pain in my hips, pelvis and back. I suffer frequently with severe headaches. My numerous medications include Valium, Neurontin, Zocar, Serezone, Paxil and Adalat.

A morphine pump was surgically implanted to give me the dose of medicine continually needed to control my excruciating pain. I visited many doctors through the years, including Orthopedists and Neurosurgeons. When I inquired with my medical doctor about chiropractic as a treatment to relieve my pain, I was simply told "no". Eventually, I became tired of dealing with the pain and decided to make an appointment with a Chiropractor. Since beginning chiropractic care, my pain has improved greatly. I was able to sleep through the night instead of waking up every half hour. Not only was I sleeping better, my pain was decreased and I was able to do more activities without experiencing the excruciating pain. In the next few months, I believed that I would experience additional physical benefits and see continued progress in my health. At one point, during the course of my chiropractic care, I was feeling so good that my medical doctor and I discussed having the morphine pump removed.

After my first month of treatment, my progress was so great that I was able to move into rehabilitation exercises in Dr. Pisciottano's chiropractic office. I was still being adjusted, but I was also working on improving my flexibility and strength. No one thought I would ever be able to accomplish this. The doctors were very clear with me in the beginning of my treatment. They were going to do the best they could to help reduce my pain, but because of the extent of my injuries, they did not know the amount of long-term improvement I would achieve. I actually got to the point where I was using weight machines to help strengthen my muscles again. I am so happy that I tried Dr. Pisciottano's system of chiropractic care.

My health has changed so dramatically that I could do things after Dr. Pisciottano's Pro-Adjuster treatment that I thought I would never be able to do again. This treatment has given me a new level of performance. Thanks Dr. Pisciottano!
- BILL HARPS

We see people in our offices daily that have stories similar to Bob's and Bill's. We wonder, however about the number of people that continue to endure years of suffering and will never have the good fortune to walk into a Chiropractor's office to receive help. We wonder how many people are suffering needlessly when help, in fact, hope may be just around the corner. Thoughts come to mind of a traveler stranded in the desert who is unsure of which direction to pursue. He is lost, beaten down, famished and dehydrated, crawling in his last moments, only stopping to die a few hundred feet from water. How many people are searching for pain relief, and health, but are traveling down the wrong road? Unfortunately, the answer is in the millions.

- **16,500 people die each year due to gastrointestinal problems caused by NSAIDS.** NSAIDS are a class of readily prescribed drugs that are non-steroidal anti-inflammatory drugs. These include ibuprofen, Aleve, Naproxen, etc. This statistic may make NSAIDS the 15th most common cause of death in the U.S.!
  Source: The New England Journal of Medicine, June 16, 1999

- **35% of people are on dialysis due to the use of anti-inflammatory drugs and over-the-counter medications. 60% of people are on dialysis due to prescription medications.** 5% of people are on dialysis due to hereditary factors. Source: 1999 Internet Study

Many people are becoming wary of the drug and surgery answers to every health problem. Awareness of these types of needless drug tragedies is on the rise. As doctors we do not believe it is fast enough. We want more people to understand this problem immediately. People are dying needlessly every minute of every day. What is encouraging is the number of people who are turning away from drugs and are now seeking natural healing methods. An Internet survey completed in May 2000 by Intersurvey, Inc. shows that two-thirds of Americans have tried what is called "alternative care." Alternative care simply means care that is non-medical. The survey results showed that 37% of the respondents had received chiropractic care, and that 38% had tried herbal medicines. Interestingly, many Chiropractors utilize nutritional and herbal therapy in their practices. Doctors of chiropractic receive substantial nutritional education as part of their standard curriculum. Many continue to receive yearly continuing education and additional degrees in these areas of expertise.

Of course, there are many reasons why people seek care beyond traditional medicine, but clearly this shows that individuals are taking more responsibility for their own health by pursuing other avenues in order to enhance their health. The numerous media reports on the adverse effects of drugs and surgery surely have impacted the opinions on how we should heal.

The previously mentioned survey also showed that chiropractic care was thought to be extremely effective by the greatest number of respondents. There is nothing to indicate that these numbers will not continue to grow. People are now demanding more choices and better care. They are tired of having only two choices, drugs and surgery, neither of which are pleasant and may have numerous consequences and side effects.

This is certainly evidenced by extrapolations to the U. S. population suggesting 629 million visits to "alternative medicine" practitioners in 1997. This exceeds the total visits to all U. S. primary care physicians of only 386 million visits. The estimated expenditures were conservatively at 21.2 billion in 1997 with 12.2 billion of that being paid out of the consumers' pocket. This indicates to us that people who are educated about their healthcare choices tend to determine their own path. These people are no longer willing to follow a course set for them by their insurance carrier or medical doctor. They are willing to get the care that is the most effective for them, even though they may be responsible for payment. The survey further relays this message by clearly showing the reasons why people try non-medical or alternative health treatments. The highest percentage (62%) is a recommendation not from their medical doctor but from a friend or family member. People are beginning to question their medical professionals more carefully, and are increasingly listening to people who have had similar personal experiences and positive results with alternative care. Sadly, not enough doctors are recommending anything outside of their own medicated and surgical world. Only 22% of medical professionals will recommend to a patient that they try a non-medical approach to their treatment.

There has always been extreme power in a good result. If you knew ten people or even one person who had resolved their health problems through safe and effective, non-surgical, medication free methods, you would likely opt to use the same form of treatment if you needed it. The clinical proof of millions of people using chiropractic care safely and effectively has been available for over 100 years. The increased use of computers and the Internet has brought our world closer and more informed. Another 20% of people have tried alternatives from information they received from magazines, newspapers and Internet sources. People believe what they read, and the information gathered by the Internet is seemingly as credible as the recommendations from their doctors. Blindly trusting any one source without any investigation is never wise. For hundreds of years people did this with their physicians. We have all heard too many of these stories and reports, like women who had "routine" hysterectomies performed because their doctor "told them to." It is an awakening that everyone must be fully educated to the choices of healthcare before us. To weigh the consequences of our actions and know fully what our outcomes may be. Only then can we make rational choices that serve our best interest.

Chiropractic is an effective means of handling many health problems related to nerve impingement. Many people do not realize the impact that the nervous system has on our total health. Simply put, the nerves are the electricity to the entire body. In the event that there is even a slight compromise in the flow of the "electricity" to the body, complications can occur. Muscles do not function to their full capacities. Organs may malfunction. Pain may result. No one treatment can be effective for all people at all times. Your doctor of chiropractic, armed with the Pro-Adjuster technology and the other natural treatment choices may be able to have a greater overall impact on your health than any other type of treatment or therapy. The Pro-Adjuster is so precise and engineered very specifically so that it can deliver the best possible outcomes. It takes some of the individual judgment out of the equation. We believe that future studies will show an enormous increase in the amount of people using chiropractic care because of the effectiveness and results of the Pro-Adjuster equipment. Will this make manual treatments obsolete? No, but this technology is a great advancement in the ability to treat a patient safely, with great results and in a short period of time. Some form of manual treatment may also be indicated however now your doctor has more options for you. Can an automobile be analyzed, checked and tuned up without high tech equipment? Of course it can. However, by utilizing having the new sophisticated instruments available to precisely fine tune and analyze every aspect of your engine means an even better and more finely tuned vehicle. This is exactly what we want for our vehicles and we should expect no less for our bodies. After all we have to use our bodies for an entire lifetime. It is the vehicle that carries our life force from beginning to end.

Why not treat it like it was a Ferrari?

I first came to Dr. Pisciottano on January 3, 2000. I was introduced to the office through a friend. I was diagnosed with degenerative spine disease in 1999. I had trouble walking, sitting, bending, standing, and could not drive. I had been using muscle relaxants and anti-inflammatory drugs to reduce swelling and pain. Everything I had been trying did not work. My PCP advised me to try chiropractic care. I now feel great thanks to the Pro-Adjuster. The pain I had been experiencing is minimal. The greatest surprise is that my migraines have gone from weekly to once a month and sometimes none at all.

-ALICE BOCK

Chapter Four

Assessing Your Health

"Take good care of your future because that's where you're going to spend the rest of your life."

-K. KETTERING

Before you can decide whether you should visit a Chiropractor for pain relief or just a simple checkup, it is imperative that you understand what a Chiropractor looks for and why. Spinal health is one of the most vital aspects of your total health that should be assessed and cared for. Understanding some basic concepts will aid your ability to make informed decisions regarding your health. There are two main reasons why anyone would seek out any type of doctor. The first is because the person is in pain. Let's face it, most people do not enjoy going to doctors and dentists if they don't have to. Pain is a great motivator. If a person is in severe enough pain or continual pain they will seek help. By the time you are finished with this book you will understand why waiting to be in pain before taking action is a mistake. The second reason people go to a doctor is for checkups such as blood pressure, heart, cholesterol, mammogram, dental, eye, etc. Although awareness is greater for these routine exams, very few people understand the vital importance of having their nervous system evaluated and treated. In this information age, a time of people searching for the answers to increased longevity, all that is about to change. Many of our patients have this understanding and are experiencing better health performance without the risks of drugs. Very few people go to their medical doctor asking for disease prevention and wellness programs designed to aid them throughout their lives. In the last few years certain doctors and hospitals have been shifting gears and talking about prevention and wellness. People still do not understand the entire concept because they are approaching the subject from a drug and surgery oriented perspective: that medical model of thinking. Doctors of chiropractic have been involved in prevention, wellness, nutrition and pain relief for over one hundred years. Wellness and ultimate health must start by means of the body's natural ability to be healthy. Even as little as fifty years ago, people did not evaluate their teeth or other systems as thoroughly or routinely as now. Can you imagine nowadays if a person ignored their teeth and allowed dental decay to overtake them? What if blood pressure and cholesterol weren't checked? It is so straightforward to have these things done routinely, and it is very smart to do so. It is always better to prevent problems or catch a potential risk early on. Our focus in this book is to elevate your awareness. Understand the critical value of improved spinal health and make a decision that can have a positive impact on you and your family.

Great emphasis has been placed on heart function and cholesterol levels. In other words, a heightened attentiveness exists about treating the heart and vascular system correctly from diet, exercise and possible medical intervention. Most everyone seems to understand that once your heart is overtaxed and your blood vessels are too clogged up there is a great possibility for life to end. As important as this cardiovascular system is, clearly a system exists that is superior to it in importance and function. This is the nervous system. Comprised of your master control center—the brain and all the "electrical wiring" that links every organ and tissue of the body together, the nerves. As critical as the heart is, for getting the blood pumped through our blood vessels and taking nutrients to every body part, so is the brain that consistently sends signals to it via the nerves commanding it to operate. In the event that the nerve supply to the heart was impaired severely, the heart may cease to function. This would also be true with every organ's function in the body.

Globally, people learned the importance of proper nervous system function as they watched the story of actor Christopher Reeves unfold. He played Superman in the movies. A horseback riding accident damaged his spinal cord in a very dramatic way and the consequences have been profound. It is clear that much of his body within a short period of time began to malfunction and degenerate. The vitality of his body, his health and proper function rests solely on the ability of his nervous system to transmit the proper signals throughout his body. It is a critical and complex system that science and doctors continue to learn more about daily. There is also a basic simple fact that if one can grasp and remember, will make true sense on a very basic, instinctive level. This is called innate intelligence; The wisdom that our bodies know what is right. Breaking down the complexity of spinal anatomy, neurology, and physiology into a simple, usable and reproducible idea would go something like this. The brain controls and regulates every system, organ, cell and tissue in the body through the nerves. The nerves are our wiring system with hundreds of thousands of nerves running throughout the body. They transmit chemical and electrical impulses to tell the body how to function. If they can do this without interruption from outside influences, then the body would have the ability to function at a near perfect state, which we can call health. But if the nervous system is assaulted or interfered with, it will either not be able to send a signal at all or only send a partial signal to its final destination. This might be a muscle, an adrenal gland, the stomach or another organ or tissue. The nervous system can be assaulted through the obvious such as direct and severe trauma as was the case with Christopher Reeves.

Trauma can come from many sources such as a fall or auto, sports, or work injury. The nervous system can be injured or interfered with slowly over time from other physical interferences of our daily lives, lifting, bending, twisting, poor posture, etc. It can be damaged from chemical sources also either too much or too little of something. Too little might be the lack of proper nutrition to feed the nerves maybe eating too much junk food or not getting the proper vitamins such as B-vitamins through supplementation. Perhaps the system is being bombarded with chemicals from a job, the air, the water or medications, even the additives and preservatives that are introduced to our foods. The nerves can be slowly damaged over time from any of these things and you may not even realize it until many symptoms start to present themselves. The vertebrae, which protect and surround the spinal cord and the nerve roots, can themselves be an immediate or progressive source of interference with the proper functioning of the nerves. This can manifest slowly due to bodily assaults chemically or physically or can be abrupt or immediate through trauma. The proper functioning of the nervous system, sending signals down the nerve pathways is critical to our health. Therefore, an evaluation of spinal health is something everyone should have, whether to determine proper function of the individual, or especially to ascertain what effects that previous trauma has had on the nervous system. Let's face it; all of us have had one or more event happen to us during our lives. We just haven't realized, maybe until right now the full impact of these episodes on the functionality of our bodies. The following flow chart may make it clearer to you. Remember that the master plan is that our bodies should function at 100% and the brain should control 100% of the body 100% of the time.

These life situations impede the bodies' ability to function at an optimum state:

- **100% Function (optimum state of being)**
  - Birth (80% of births are traumatic)
  - Childhood falls
    (47% of all children fall on their head by age 1) (OSHA)
  - Children aged 2 to 5 fall at least 200 times
  - 12 Years of Poor Posture in School
  - Teenage Stress
  - Car Accidents
    (70% of teenagers are in an accident within 2 years of receiving their license)
  - College stress
  - Diet-Junk Food
  - Occupational Stress
  - Failure to exercise
  - Relationship stress
  - Financial Stress
  - **40% Function**
    (possible symptom stage after years of abuse)

Is it possible that your body may not be functioning as well as you believed? These are probably all new ideas for you. A vast portion of the population has had so many things happen to them throughout their lives that it is no wonder there is so much ill health throughout the world. Consider the one statistic of 80% of births being traumatic. Many times the delivering doctor must break the baby's clavicle and forcibly turn the head as much as 180° to remove the child from the birth canal. Forceps may be utilized as can suction devices to the top of the baby's head. These procedures can be damaging to a newborn. This is the welcome to the world many of us have had. Dr. Suh at the University of Colorado found that it only takes about 10 mm of mercury pressure (about what you would feel holding a dime in your hand) to interfere with nerve transmission as much as sixty percent! How much pressure do you think has been applied to your nerves throughout your life? A person may wonder why they continually become sick, but have never been told how vital the nervous system is, or how it can be the source of many health problems.

Some of the most common symptoms indicating a nervous system overload are the following:

- Headaches   • Fatigue   • Sleep Disturbances
- Sinus and Allergies   • Pain   • Mood Swings

Are you currently suffering from any of these? If so, for how long? Think back and remember a time when you didn't have these problems. Then look at what has changed or occurred that created this problem for you. Seriously stop and take a look at this. Use the following guide to search your life for possible clues. You may be surprised to find that after a trauma perhaps even years later you developed some health problems. Don't be frustrated if you can't remember. Sometimes it takes weeks or months before a memory resurfaces. In fact, other family members may remember something you don't. For example, we had a patient who fell out of a fast moving car at the age of four. She didn't remember this at all during her consultation. But during a family discussion, her mom told her about it. She had never known! She then realized that the headaches she had been suffering with for over 26 years started after that trauma! Try to find out when your problems started. Write down anything you may recall.

0-5 years of age: _____

5-10 years of age: _____

10-15 years of age: _____

15-20 years of age: _____

20-30 years of age: _____

30-40 years of age: _____

40-50 years of age: _____

50+ years of age: _____

You may not instantly remember or even realize the answers right now. But come back to this later and don't forget to quiz the family. However, even if you can't determine why, it is more important to realize you have a problem that needs attention now, and then take action to resolve it!

Let's evaluate the status of your health further. We want to see whether you are prone to lower productivity, loss of energy or spinal related injury. Please answer the following questions and place a check mark next to those that apply.

Yes   No

Do you have restricted range of motion in the

☐   ☐   Cervical (neck)

☐   ☐   Thoracic (back)

☐   ☐   Lumbar (low back)

If yes, is it in the:

☐   ☐   Morning

☐   ☐   Afternoon

☐   ☐   Evening

☐   ☐   You feel tired, fatigued or just out of fuel one time per day or more.

☐   ☐   You already have pains in cervical, thoracic and lumbar areas.

Yes	No	
☐	☐	You require coffee or soda in morning to "Get Started."
☐	☐	You are overweight or are out of condition.
☐	☐	You find yourself "day dreaming" during the work day.
☐	☐	You have had spinal or carpal tunnel surgery.
☐	☐	You go home from work feeling like you have not accomplished enough or anything.
☐	☐	You have been told you have arthritis.
☐	☐	You feel you are under the physical effects of stress-work, home, financial, marital, etc.
☐	☐	You have more than 3 or 4 headaches per year.
☐	☐	You consume Aspirin, Advil, Ibuprofen, Dones, Tylenol, Muscle Relaxers, Toridol, Prozac, Zoloft, etc. so you can feel better.
☐	☐	You have been involved in a motor vehicle accident—even one— in your lifetime.

By now you should be forming a rather good picture of your health status. This is the time to be totally honest and take a good look in the mirror. Is your health as good as you thought it was? Did you gain insight about your health? Do you think it could be improved? Have you been minimizing problems? If you have discovered that you have answered yes to more than one of those questions, then perhaps it is time to take action to become healthier. We suggest that if even one yes box was checked off you should be evaluated to determine the cause and if it could become a more serious problem later. You must become an informed keeper of your health. Then make a conscious decision to take action. Next take the action step necessary to resolve the problem. We have found that each one of those yes boxes can be handled through chiropractic and nutritional intervention by balancing the body physically and chemically. It may be easier than you think.

To help you get one step closer to making a decision we have included some nerve distribution charts. Neuroanatomy is a highly complex topic because nerve pathways are sophisticated and intricate. It would be overwhelming to attempt to diagram and correlate it to your potential problem areas. However, having a basic idea of nerve pathways will direct you to a potential problem area of your spine based on your symptoms. This is a guide to help you understand the overall impact that irritation, injury, or pressure on the nervous system can have on your health. This is an invaluable tool in assessing your health concerns. It is important to note that irritation to spinal nerves may cause symptoms later. So not having a symptom is not a valid indicator of nervous system health. Be aware of potential future problems. Put a check mark next to the symptoms that apply to you. We suggest further in depth analysis of your problems be considered, and urge you to have a nervous system evaluation performed.

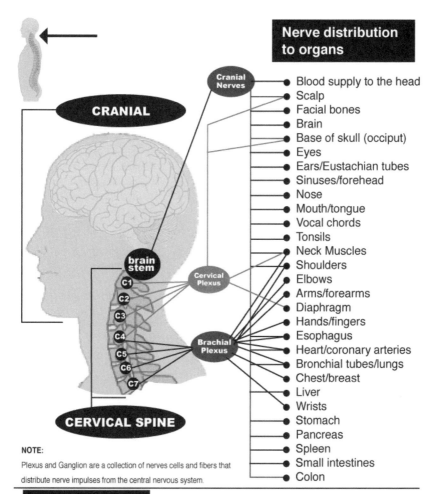

Nerve distribution to organs

- Blood supply to the head
- Scalp
- Facial bones
- Brain
- Base of skull (occiput)
- Eyes
- Ears/Eustachian tubes
- Sinuses/forehead
- Nose
- Mouth/tongue
- Vocal chords
- Tonsils
- Neck Muscles
- Shoulders
- Elbows
- Arms/forearms
- Diaphragm
- Hands/fingers
- Esophagus
- Heart/coronary arteries
- Bronchial tubes/lungs
- Chest/breast
- Liver
- Wrists
- Stomach
- Pancreas
- Spleen
- Small intestines
- Colon

CRANIAL

brain stem

Cranial Nerves

Cervical Plexus

Brachial Plexus

C1 C2 C3 C4 C5 C6 C7

CERVICAL SPINE

NOTE:
Plexus and Ganglion are a collection of nerves cells and fibers that distribute nerve impulses from the central nervous system.

Signs/symptoms possible effects from nervous system interference

Headaches/including-
-migraines
Fatigue
Chronic tiredness
Sinus problems
Allergies
Shoulder, arm, wrist, hand and
fingers-pain & or numbness
& tingling

Dizziness
Muscular aches/ pains
Stiff neck
Muscle spasms
Burning sensations on skin
or muscles
Head colds
Vision problems
Hearing
Common cold
Runny nose
Sore throat
Croup
Tennis elbow

Tonsillitis
Hoarseness
Laryngitis
Cough
Shortness of breath
Breathing problems
Asthma
Chest pains
Heart conditions
Heartburn
Bed wetting

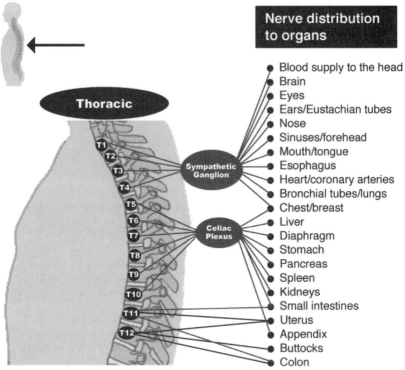

Nerve distribution to organs

Thoracic

Sympathetic Ganglion

Celiac Plexus

- Blood supply to the head
- Brain
- Eyes
- Ears/Eustachian tubes
- Nose
- Sinuses/forehead
- Mouth/tongue
- Esophagus
- Heart/coronary arteries
- Bronchial tubes/lungs
- Chest/breast
- Liver
- Diaphragm
- Stomach
- Pancreas
- Spleen
- Kidneys
- Small intestines
- Uterus
- Appendix
- Buttocks
- Colon

NOTE:

Plexus and Ganglion are a collection of nerves cells and fibers that distribute nerve impulses from the central nervous system.

Signs/symptoms possible effects from nervous system interference

Headaches/ including migraines
Fatigue
Dizziness
Chronic tiredness
Sinus problems
Allergies
Shoulder, arm, wrist, hand and fingers-pain & or numbness & tingeling
Muscular aches/ pains
Stiff neck
Muscle spasms
Burning sensations on skin or muscles

Head colds
Vision problems
Hearing
Common cold
Runny nose
Sore throat
Croup
Tennis elbow
Tonsillitis
Hoarseness
Laryngitis
Cough
Shortness of breath
Breathing problems
Asthma
Chest pains
Heart conditions
Heartburn
Bed wetting

Bronchitis
Pheumonia, congestion
Hiatal hernia
Gallbladder conditions
Blood pressure problems
Liver conditions
Jaundice
Skin conditions,acne
Stomach troubles
Indigestion
GastritisHeartburn
Gas pains
Ulcers
Blood sugar problems
Kidney conditions
Chronic tiredness
Constipation, diarrhea

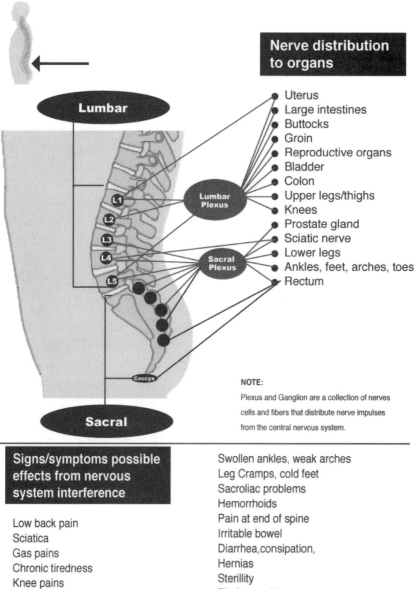

Nerve distribution to organs

- Uterus
- Large intestines
- Buttocks
- Groin
- Reproductive organs
- Bladder
- Colon
- Upper legs/thighs
- Knees
- Prostate gland
- Sciatic nerve
- Lower legs
- Ankles, feet, arches, toes
- Rectum

Lumbar

Lumbar Plexus

Sacral Plexus

L1
L2
L3
L4
L5

Coccyx

Sacral

NOTE:

Plexus and Ganglion are a collection of nerves cells and fibers that distribute nerve impulses from the central nervous system.

Signs/symptoms possible effects from nervous system interference

Low back pain
Sciatica
Gas pains
Chronic tiredness
Knee pains
Muscular aches/ pains
Muscle spasms
Burning sensations on skin or muscles
Numbness, tingling,poor circulation in legs
Shin splints

Swollen ankles, weak arches
Leg Cramps, cold feet
Sacroliac problems
Hemorrhoids
Pain at end of spine
Irritable bowel
Diarrhea,consipation,
Hernias
Sterillity
Bladder problems
Menstrual problems, cramps
Bed wetting
Difficult or painful urination

Now that you have taken the quizzes, answered the questions, checked off the boxes and followed the nerve supply, how did you do? There is another simple test to see whether your nervous system might be impaired and functioning in less than an adequate way. First, while standing, raise one foot off the ground lifting your knee towards your chest. You should be able to balance without much difficulty and you should definitely not fall over. Next, while in that same position, close your eyes. Again you should be able to maintain balance. How did you do? Next, stand in front of a light switch and with one hand, index finger extended, reach out and touch the switch. Then repeat this action, and this time keep your eyes closed. You should be able to touch the light switch with your eyes closed as well as open. Now, repeat this procedure with the other hand. How did you do? Your nervous system is designed to keep you in balance. You should be able to duplicate an action. If you couldn't perform these tests or you performed them poorly, then this is quite likely a nervous system problem. Remember, the nervous system is the secret to health, healing, pain relief and longevity. If it is not functioning properly a host of health problems can occur.

If you made it through the various surveys, symptom charts, and tests without checking off any boxes or failing any parts, then congratulations! You are probably in great health! You are then challenged to have a family member or friend do the same tests. Chances are you know someone who may not do so well. If that is the case please share these tests with them. They will then be exposed to the knowledge, and can have the opportunity to take a good look at their health condition and get help that is necessary to change their life. If you checked off even one of the boxes or failed a question or two, then your body is sending signals that there is a problem. Your nervous system absolutely needs to be evaluated. Do not take your spinal health for granted. Get to your chiropractic doctor now! You need your spine aligned to remove nervous system pressure. By adjusting the spine the nerves are able to freely express their energy. Your body will then be able to repair itself and can achieve better function. We have the right solution for you.

After attending a Peak Performance lecture, I realized that the problems I was having were something that I didn't have to live with. I had been experiencing several problems. The worst of which were migraine headaches that caused me to become physically ill and miss work. I tried several different over the counter drugs to deal with the headaches but those offered only temporary relief. I made an appointment for a complete evaluation in May of 2002 and became a patient at Dr. Pisciottano's. I have had tremendous results with the Pro-Adjuster. After the second treatment, the headaches were gone! I also have a lot more energy and feel much stronger.

- KATHLEEN FLEISSNER

Chapter Five

Pro-Adjuster — A Breakthrough in Healing

"There is one thing stronger than all the armies in the world: an idea whose time has come." -VICTOR HUGO

Imagine thirty to forty years ago, if we told you that dentistry would be painless, that doctors would watch television to perform surgeries, that brain surgery for tumors could be done with a laser, that fetuses could be operated on within the uterus, that knife-less surgery could be performed — you would not have believe us. By the same token, would you believe us if we told you that chiropractic manipulations and reorientation of the nervous system could be done *painlessly* without any popping or cracking sounds, and no jerking or pulling of the body or neck? Would you believe that newborns as well as the elderly with osteoporosis could be treated effortlessly? The facts are all these things that were never heard of before, perhaps once just dreams in someone's head are now reality and commonplace procedures. The future is now! Advances in computers and engineering technology have been able to uniquely blend with chiropractic in order to both analyze and treat the human body in such a way that was never before realized. The potential for the human being to end pain and to achieve their peak nervous system enhancement has never been greater. Humans are consistently asking their bodies to perform at higher levels. Now we have the techniques and the technology to match the demands placed on the spine and the nervous system. We now have the capability to fine tune our own energy and enhance every aspect of our lives.

What if there was something you could do from the day you were born to extend your life, improve your performance and maximize your health? Would you do it? Of course you would! That's what people call a "no brainer." It is easy to look back on life from a new vantage point and say, "I should have done that differently." Financial experts will tell you that simply putting one dollar a day into a mutual fund will yield one million dollars in twenty years. Can you imagine that great reward by a simple daily action! How many of us look back and say, "I wish I had done that." Creating a simple daily habit can have a tremendous impact on the future. This is true of one's health also. We can create health in our bodies through some simple actions that will compound over time to pay huge health dividends! Wishing does none of us any good. Only actions will produce results. If the past can not be changed, let's alter the future. Start today by creating a new reality of your own health. Certainly we wouldn't want to wait another 5 years and say, "Wow, look at all that time we've wasted, again!" Would you? None of us can go back in time and start our finances over. In the same way, we cannot rewrite our health history. What can be accomplished however is changing the way our health will be managed for the future. There may be an opportunity with a child or grandchild, however, to create something for them from the very beginning. All of us can make a conscious decision right now, in present time, to improve our health now and in the future.

The method to achieve maximum health from your body now and in the future begins with a simple anatomical concept. The nervous system (the brain and all the nerves) controls every function of your body. If this network is interfered with, pain ensues as bodily malfunction does, resulting in sickness and diminished overall health. That "something" you can do to improve performance and maximize health is to maximize the health of your nervous system. There are several ways to do this. The number one way is allowing a doctor of chiropractic using the Pro-Adjuster equipment to analyze and treat your nervous system.

Several hundred years B.C. Hippocrates advised that the spine should be looked at and evaluated as the source of many diseases. This ancient wisdom is increasingly applicable today. Your spine consists of a "backbone" (column of spinal vertebrae) and the nervous system, the spinal cord and spinal nerves that exit through openings between the vertebrae. Twenty-four bones are stacked up one on top of the other from your skull down to your tailbone. Muscles and ligaments are attached to these bones for movement and stability.

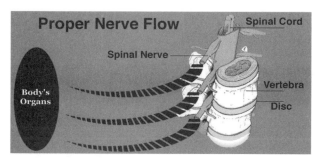

A *vertebral motor unit* consists of one vertebra on top of another separated by a soft cushion called a disc. A hole is formed by the shape and positioning of the two vertebrae. This hole allows the spinal nerves to pass through unobstructed. The nerve roots send electrical and nutritional energy to every organ and tissue of your body through millions of nerve fibers.

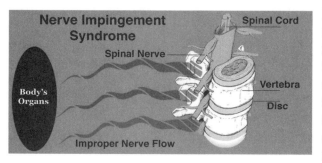

If the vertebrae are misaligned in some way they will be unable to move and function as designed, thereby creating aberrant motion. These misaligned vertebrae are termed subluxations, fixations or motion defects. These fixations/motion defects create a situation where the vertebrae may be rigid (hypo-mobile) or too fluid (hyper-mobile.) The end result is *Nerve Impingement Syndrome*. Ultimately this translates to nervous system interference resulting in pain or ill health without pain. It interferes or stops the flow of electrical information from being successfully passed through, the "flow is impeded". Impedance is simply something that is blocking another thing. Just as traffic accidents would impede the flow of vehicles. Traffic would pass through an area where an accident has occurred more slowly with few vehicles at a time. Another example of this would be a dam which impedes the flow of water.

Cars (Backed Up) Accident

Less Traffic

A dam impedes flow.

Free flowing stream.

The nervous system is the electrical wiring of your body that allows you to perform. Much like the wiring of your house allows lights to function and perform at optimum levels. Visualize a standard dimmer switch in your house. By turning the switch you can create more impedance to the electrical flow. By doing this, it is demonstrated easily that less electricity traveling to your light bulb means less light. Therefore there is less than optimum performance produced from the bulb. It is capable of more but can not give it because of the impedance. When they are misaligned, the vertebrae and discs can act like a dimmer switch impeding nerve flow, creating malfunction, ill health and poor performance from the body.

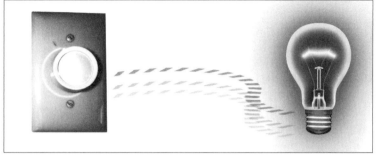

Dimmer Switch and Light bulb

This situation can successfully be treated using the Pro-Adjuster. Restoring proper motion of the vertebrae with the Pro-Adjuster results in less impedance to the spinal nerves, resulting in improved, proper nervous system function, resulting in improved bodily performance, resulting in improved health!

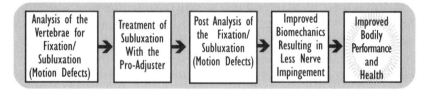

How does the Pro-Adjuster work? To better understand let's examine the idea of palpation. Traditionally, without the Pro-Adjuster, the Chiropractor uses a technique called *palpation* to determine the location of subluxations within an individual's spine. These subluxations feel rigid or stiff. It takes much discipline and practice to become proficient at determining the level or degree that a vertebra is fixated. Although all Chiropractors are highly skilled in palpation, there is no way to determine scientifically or mathematically how much rigidity exists in the vertebral unit. In order to get the sense of palpation, push down on some hard surface, the wall or a tabletop for example. You will notice these objects are very rigid. They do not move. Now push on something like a pillow or a couch cushion and note that there is less rigidity. This will give you some idea of how the Chiropractor, when he or she is palpating your spine, is checking for joint fluidity, motion, and or rigidity. More specifically, they would be checking for subluxations. The spine should not be too rigid (hypo-mobile) nor should it be too flexible (hyper-mobile.) In a similar fashion to palpation, the Pro-Adjuster can determine whether the vertebra is too rigid or too fluid. However, instead of utilizing the doctor's judgment as to what is hypo-mobile or hyper-mobile, the Pro-Adjuster measures *precise* levels of fixation. Therefore, the Pro-Adjuster can isolate a problem area faster and more accurately than any of us can do manually. Following examination with the Pro-Adjuster, the doctor will then determine the correct treatment to be applied. The way the Pro-Adjuster instrument determines whether the vertebra is too rigid or too fluid is by applying a light mechanical force to the spine directly through the patient's clothing. When a doctor is palpating a person's spine by applying hands on pressure, the body goes into a normal defense (posture/mechanism). It causes the muscles to contract and guard against an impact. If you have ever "flinched" at something you know exactly what this means. The piezoelectric crystal in the Pro-Adjuster instrument responds and registers information faster than your body's ability to respond. Therefore, a precise and accurate picture of the extent of rigidity or fluidity of the vertebrae is reflected. In other words, a signal is sent into the vertebrae to check motion, it is reflected back to the piezoelectric crystal, which measures the reflective force, sending it to the computer for interpretation all before the muscle can respond in its normal way. Isn't that incredible? This is the same technology and same type instrument that NASA engineers have used in the space program in order to evaluate the integrity of the ceramic cooling tiles on the outside of the space shuttle. The aviation industries, as well as the civil engineering industry have used this technology in order to test metal fatigue in aircraft and bridge spans. Chiropractors are now able to use this highly sophisticated technology applied to the human body in order to determine proper function. We can have the same level of care given to our bodies as multimillion-dollar spacecraft. Doesn't that give you a sense of being special and give you a higher level of confidence?

Placing this sensitive instrument at each vertebral level of the spine, the doctor will apply a very slight pressure. The piezoelectric head coupled to the computer runs a highly sophisticated program. The instrument will accurately and comfortably measure the resistance of the vertebrae of your spine and record the data.

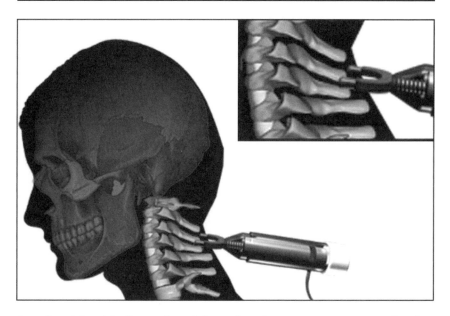

An algorithm* is formulated in order that a treatment can be designed. The computer screen will display a waveform that matches the resistance of the vertebrae. A normal vertebra would produce a symmetrical bell- shaped waveform. A dysfunctional vertebral joint will produce erratic or aberrant wave forms. They may be too high, too low, or asymmetrical.

These waveforms indicate to the doctor the area and type of malfunction. It can be determined whether the vertebrae are fixated (rigid or stiff, or in other words, stuck). This is called hypomobility. If the joint being measured is too fluid or mobile (loose), this is called hypermobility. If the vertebral segment is too loose it will lack stability. Therefore treating around this area would strengthen it. The next time the spinal segments are tested the test

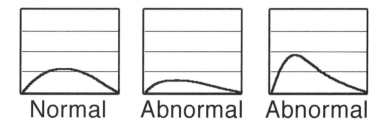

*Algorithm-interprets a series of formulas or data and then gives the answer, much like a translator listening to 15 people speaking 15 different languages. Imagine if that were funneled into a device that could take the information and translate it into one language that everyone could understand.

should show a definite improvement. The doctor based on their extensive understanding of Biomechanics, Neurology, Physiology, Anatomy, Histology, Palpation, and spinal adjusting must properly interpret this information. Your qualified Pro-Adjuster doctor will then determine the appropriate treatment.

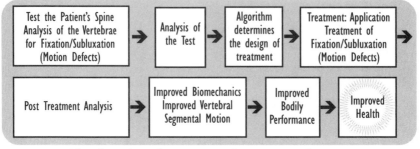

This flow chart demonstrates the sequence of events.

Once the testing for rigidity or fluidity is complete, a rigidity number is then determined. The computer analyzes and "says" basically, "You need to tap on the vertebrae so many times in a precise and controlled way until less rigidity is realized." The doctor can now apply the treatment via the percussive instrument using a very light and steady pressure. Once enough treatment has been determined, a result is then realized. When the computer registers 10 consecutive "taps" that are measured equally, it knows that the vertebrae is less rigid and automatically stops the percussion. The treatment is then complete. We have reached the desired result! Think of the procedure this way. Picture a door that you would have to open to pass through. In the event that the door is stuck when you push on it, you will meet a certain amount of resistance or rigidity. This is not normal because the door as a mechanical device with hinges should open freely. Imagine if you could measure the amount of resistance that door was giving you. This can then be compared to the Pro Adjuster's ability to accurately measure the resistance of the vertebrae within your spine. As you put your shoulder to the door and push on it, there will still be resistance. With enough pressure, and by pushing long enough, with the correct amount of force, the immobile door would eventually free up and open. At this point you would stop pushing because the door would be freely moving. There is no need to continue because the job is done. This is what the Pro-Adjuster will do as it percusses. Once the sensor in the instrument registers less resistance, it automatically ceases operation. In doing so, you and the doctor will know when the adjustment is complete. This ensures that no excess treatment is performed. This is why the treatment is safe, pain free and accurate. The doctor can then reevaluate the spine with the instrument and a post analysis will be displayed on the screen. You will then be able to see the degree of change and actually compare the before and after readings. Further treatment can be determined from that point by the doctor. Each treatment will build on the last because each and every visit will involve a new analysis of the spine, then treatment, a post analysis, and then visual education to the patient. The body (unlike the door) is a living organism hence it goes through an improvement phase. Just as lifting weights one time does not build a big muscle, one time slightly moving a vertebra that has likely been subluxated for years, will not correct the problem. In the same way, pushing through that difficult door the next time is not as hard, next time the Pro-Adjuster analyzes the vertebral segment it will not be as bad, nor will it meet as much resistance. There will be steady improvement until ultimately the problem is resolved. The outcome will be improved motion, enhanced nerve response, better bodily function, and superior performance!

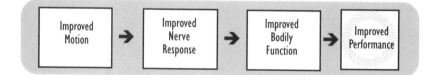

Hopefully you now realize how spinal misalignments (subluxations) may be the underlying cause of many of your health problems without you even knowing it! Only 7% of nerve fibers in the body carry pain signals, the other 93% do not; therefore you may not know you have subluxations. You may not even be experiencing pain or other symptoms while your system is malfunctioning because of nerve impingement syndrome. This is why it is vital to your health to have your nervous system function checked. The Pro-Adjuster is the ideal instrument for this process, and is used only by the doctor who is fully capable of analyzing and treating your nervous system — the Chiropractor.

My very first visit to Dr. Pisciottano was on March 21, 2002. I had been having a lot of neck and back pain with a restricted range of motion. I learned of the Pro-Adjuster at the health club I attend and decided to check it out. I previously went through chiropractic treatment with some results, however, the idea of having my bones cracked and pushed on made me very nervous. The Pro-Adjuster just made sense to me. I didn't have to be worried because the treatment was totally painless! I am currently going through the rehabilitation portion that is offered here at the clinic, strengthening my muscles and reducing the risk of re-injuring my spine. The movement in my neck has returned and my back feels great!

- UTE PHILLIP

Chapter Six

One Size Fits All

"You can't build health on what you are going to do tomorrow, but it can be built on what you do today."

-DR. R. F. BARRETT

Chiropractors and their patients know that manual adjustments are safe and effective, regardless of what technique is used, as long as the practitioner has the knowledge and skill to apply the method properly. However, sometimes people who have never experienced a chiropractic treatment may be fearful because of something they have seen, read or been told about what they might see, feel or experience with a chiropractic treatment. Occasionally people have a fear of the unfamiliar. With the use of the Pro-Adjuster equipment and techniques, virtually all of these fears simply disappear. If you are looking for the perfect spinal analysis, the perfect treatment, and the perfect adjustment—one that is on target, precise, and easy on the body every time—one that is painless, with no popping or cracking noises, yet highly effective, then the Pro-Adjuster is the ideal solution for you.

The Pro-Adjuster also allows the Chiropractor the ability to treat any size patient. Strength of the doctor is not a factor in this method of treatment. The Pro-Adjuster is fast, accurate, reproducible and produces phenomenal results! Occasionally people have hidden fears that they never verbalize but that may inhibit them from seeking care. Many times they are comfort issues. For example, a person who is very large or overweight may worry because they fear the doctor would have to use too much force based upon their size. With the use of the Pro-Adjuster, an exact measured percussive force treats the spine painlessly, and consequently no excessive manual force is needed. It is absolutely comfortable. Some patients have had reservations about being treated because they thought they would need to be in a hospital type gown for treatment to expose the skin. This also is an unfounded fear, as the Pro-Adjuster allows a patient to be fully clothed to receive treatments. Normal clothing does not interfere with the ability of the Pro-Adjuster to analyze or adjust the spine. In actuality, patients are so at ease that treatments can be performed openly without having to be behind closed doors. Many patients enjoy bringing friends or family members to witness (to view the treatment) and watch the changes unfold on the computer monitor. Patients who have difficulty or are uncomfortable laying face down on a typical chiropractic treatment table will enjoy the ability to sit upright in a slightly forward posture with their face cradled gently on a padded cushion.

The amount of force (pressure) that the Pro-Adjuster uses to make an adjustment of your spine is about equivalent to the tapping of your fingers on a table. Let's test this out. Put your hand flat on a table or even on your leg. Now tap your fingers as though you were listening to music that you really enjoyed. Now tap as hard as you can. That is about the amount of pressure you will feel with a Pro-Adjuster treatment! Do you think you can handle that? Of course you can. Even small children and babies can be adjusted with the Pro-Adjuster. The amount of pressure can be completely controlled and adjusted for the patient's comfort, even to accommodate those small patients and children. Another concern that comes up is about brittle bones — such as with osteoporosis. Again, the amount of force can be as the lightest fingertip pressure while tapping your fingers. The doctor who evaluates a person with that type of spinal condition will know best. This is precisely the perfect instrument for those fragile types of patients.

How can anything so gentle with such little force involved move my vertebra and change my spine? The Pro-Adjuster utilizes a precise oscillating force with uninterrupted motion. It is able to increase the mobility of the spinal segments by reducing or eliminating the fixations. In other words, the Pro Adjuster is "unsticking" the joint. Have you ever seen a woodpecker tapping in an oscillating fashion on a tree? It is hard to believe, but you can watch them bore right through the hardest wood! The Pro-Adjuster taps in much the same way but uses soft tips that are comfortable to the human body and do not create damage.

As you can see, the benefits of using the Pro Adjuster are far reaching. The accuracy and ease of analysis combined with the advanced treatment options are a huge step forward. You will be a well-educated patient understanding the full extent of spinal misalignments. The computer analysis will display your problem areas and show the organs and tissues that can be affected. You will understand the extent of your problem, how your course of treatment is proceeding and the degree of resolution of your condition. In other words, you will not be left in the dark as to your health care. Some patients don't really want to know the how or why behind their condition. They simply want to be fixed. If you are the type of individual with the purpose of really enjoying the understanding how things work, then this equipment and type of chiropractic treatment is for you. Would you like to understand your treatments better? Would you actually like to see some concrete proof of your results? Would you like the ability to measure your progress and know when your care is complete based on objective findings? You can with the Pro-Adjuster method of chiropractic treatment.

Not only is the Pro-Adjuster great for you the patient, but it is also great for your doctor. It is a valuable tool providing vital information about your spinal health, ultimately resulting in a higher level of care for you. What is it that every doctor wants for their patients and what every patient wants from their doctor? The answer is one word...RESULTS! The more the doctor knows about a patient the better the result they can give. The more a patient knows and understands about their condition, the better their result will be!

In March of 2002, I injured my back while acting in a play at church. It was shortly after that when I saw Dr. Pisciottano's Clinic commercial on T.V. I decided to check it out and I am glad that I did. The doctors here were able to find and correct the problems I was having. The Pro-Adjuster immediately made sense to me. Just the mere thought of being manually manipulated while in so much pain, scared me. With the Pro-Adjuster there was no pain. My experience here at Dr. Pisciottano's has been great. The staff are very friendly and not one of my questions were unanswered.

- STEVE NEWMAN

Chapter Seven

Moveable versus Immovable

"Changing the inner attitude of your mind can change the outer aspect of your life."   -ANONYMOUS

Evidence shows there is a growing number of people who are movable and on the move. But sadly many are still immovable. Which one are you? Benjamin Franklin said, "All mankind is divided into three classes; those who are immovable; those who are movable; and those who move. These powerful words applied to our own health can give us a glimpse of our own character and an opportunity to perhaps act differently if need be. Let's look at it. Those who are immovable — no logical, rationale or reasonable proof will force this person to change their life and improve their health condition. The truth of this is revealed by mountains of evidence showing that alcohol, tobacco, lack of exercise, and excessive fats are damaging to one's health. Yet alcoholism, obesity and tobacco addictions are huge national problems. Heart disease, cancers, and strokes are the top three killers of all Americans. We know that heart disease and some cancers can be caused by smoking. Yet enormous amounts of people ignore the truth and by continuing their "bad habits" cause immeasurable sickness and disease resulting in vast medical costs, suffering and early death. We have all heard stories of alcoholics dying from liver disease and are still unwilling to give up alcohol. Also, we all know someone who just had his coronary bypass who still wants to smoke cigarettes and does! These people flaunt their destructive behavior in the face of rational and sane thinking. No one can tell them to do anything different. No one can force them to change their actions. Not even at the cost to their families who love them so much! They are immovable!

Those who are movable — are open to suggestions, new thoughts and ideas when presented with reason, facts or new data they are able to then take a new action. These people are the ones who are willing to change, given the right set of circumstances and rationale. They may need some help or guidance but they do come around and make a decision to change. Although losing valuable time and ultimately exclaiming to themselves and others, "If only I had done this years ago! How much healthier could I have been?" It is usually a loved one who must push them into taking action for their own good. In our offices, we see that as the person who says, "My wife made the appointment and wanted me to come." They haven't fully made up their minds, but someone pushed them into action. Ultimately, this person has a positive change, and within a short period of time is a new "believer" and then promotes chiropractic heavily because of their positive experience. Usually it is the man who was moved to action, and the wife that should be thanked for taking the necessary steps to change his life.

The final group is those who move — these people are constantly seeking out better ways to improve and enhance their lives. Many baby boomers fall into this category because of their desperate attempts to stop the aging process. They do not want to get old before their time. They are interested in extending their longevity but not just for the sake of living longer, but also with the intent of being healthier and more active as they age. They are attempting to stave off disease and infirmity. Jack La Lane, although not a baby boomer, is a prime example of a person who moves. He is the original fitness guru and the epitome of health and fitness. His lifestyle is an example for all of us to strive to follow. Those who are on the move immediately accept chiropractic care and are open to the understanding of how it can benefit them not only now but also in the future. It is not only for longevity but for prevention and possible disease abatement. They understand that chiropractic is the #1 alternative health choice and does more to allow for their bodies natural abilities to heal than any other form of health care. It is these people who move that can instantaneously see and innately know that the Pro- Adjuster is the perfect new technology to treat their bodies naturally. They are not isolated to one demographic region, but are global. This is why the Pro-Adjuster is creating excitement around the world, and improving health on an international level. Japan, for example, has grasped onto this technology and the people there have accepted it as we understand and accept that everyone needs dentistry. This book is laced with stories from doctors and patients who have had remarkable results using the Pro-Adjuster technology. Dr. Masa Yamasaki practices both oriental medicine and chiropractic in Japan. He is one of the most highly respected doctors in the world in the use of instrument adjusting and has developed techniques for the Pro-Adjuster system. Patients who have been treated by Dr. Yamasaki using this technology report phenomenal results. The following is just one of many such stories.

My name is Satoko Okada and at only 36 years of age I couldn't believe the pain and trouble I would experience. One day while working at my desk on the job, I felt a loss of strength and couldn't stand up. It was very difficult to stand or walk without supporting myself on the desk or other objects to hold onto. That night the pain was so severe that it kept me awake. It was like electricity passing through the right side of my lower back. The next day I went to a bone setter that was near the company I worked for. The doctor, however, referred me to an orthopedist. Upon examination I was found to have a herniated disc. The doctor gave me a pain injection which did not help.

Walking from the doctor's office to my job I could only handle a couple of steps at a time and then I would have to stop. But finally I did make it to work, however, the acute pain interfered with my abilities to think clearly and concentrate on my job. Returning home that night all I could do was lay down to try and relieve the pain, but even that didn't help.

Several days passed and even though I was taking medication and had the pain injection I was no better. So this time the doctor gave me a different shot called an epidural block. The explanation by the doctor was that it would end the pain for a couple of days. However, it didn't even relieve the pain for one hour! I simply had to handle the pain.

Nine days later I received another epidural block but again nothing changed. The doctor said it would take a long time to cure so I should be patient. Three weeks passed since the initial onset of the condition and the pain continued.

I received yet another epidural block with again no change in my pain. I was then sent to the cooperative hospital where they performed an MRI. This showed the doctors the specific location of the herniated disc. Once again I was given an epidural block. But once again it had no affect on my pain.

They then transferred me to the pain clinic of the general hospital. The doctor at the pain clinic gave me another shot called a nerve root block. But because this too didn't work, he suggested an operation. I was in shock. But I decided against the operation.

More time passed with no change so I decided to go to Morita bone setter at Kyoto from a friend's suggestion. There I received another medical examination. The doctor said that I should go to Yamasaki chiropractic office at Kouchi and I could be cured. At this point I felt that I could only depend on God, so I decided to go to Yamasaki's office.

Before receiving any treatment, I listened to Dr. Yamasaki's story. He fully explained about the treatment procedure and his position towards it. After hearing his advice I felt I had regained the hope that had all but disappeared. My intuition told me that this doctor could help me. So, I entrusted Dr. Yamasaki with the matter of my health. Dr. Yamasaki treated my C7 vertebra with the computerized adjuster. After my first treatment on March 2nd, the acute pain with which I had been suffering since October was reduced by half!

After only the fourth treatment my pain was greatly reduced and I finally awoke in the morning refreshed. It had been a very long time since I felt that.

By the tenth day of treatment my posture was better to where I could stand almost straight up. The pain had also gotten much better and the swelling improved.

May 21st was the fourteenth day of treatment. The pain which bothered me for a long time totally disappeared. Thanks to Dr. Yamasaki my life is saved! As a matter of fact I retired from my previous office work and I am now going to a special school for drafting which has been my dream. I ride a bicycle for forty minutes every day to get to school.

In my previous circumstances I couldn't even imagine doing this. But it became possible. Now I can get a job which I would like because of Dr. Yamasaki. Now I can count on being a 100% useful person for others.

This young woman's life dramatically changed. But she spent a considerable amount of time suffering in pain. How much better could she have been had she been directed to chiropractic when her problem initially began? Can you imagine the outcome if she hadn't received chiropractic care? That is not a pleasant thought. Taking the necessary steps to appropriately handle a health problem in a timely manner is critical to the outcome. If you are one who moves, you may have already decided that chiropractic and the Pro-Adjuster technology is the right form of treatment for you. Congratulations! Don't stop reading—we promise you will love the rest of the book. By all means, make your appointment now to see and be treated by a Chiropractor who uses this advanced and revolutionary equipment. We know we don't have to worry about you procrastinating.

If you are a movable individual we know you will enjoy the rest of the book. Our goal will be to move you to a new level of understanding. You will be capable of making an informed decision that our experience tells us will change your life. Chances are that an immovable person has not even picked this book up, much less cracked the cover open to read. If they have, they may have stopped reading by now. There is a chance that a few immovable people have stuck with it. If you recognize this to be true we urge you to continue because the information is even more powerful for you. It can be like a blind person seeing for the first time. We believe that all things are possible and that anything the human mind can conceive it can achieve. Do not let misconceptions, erroneous opinions or aberrant thinking cloud your judgment and interfere with an opportunity to enhance your life, eliminate your pain or take you to a higher level of bodily performance! It is all within your grasp. Our goal is that you become movable!

I started coming to Dr. Pisciottano on March 1, 1996. I had been suffering from sinus headaches for about 6 to 8 years. They got so extreme sometimes that I had nausea and vomiting. I was previously treated by an allergist and medical doctor with only temporary relief. I have had a remarkable recovery to the point of total relief of any sinus related headaches or problems since using the Pro-Adjuster.

- CHRIS P. TATMAN

Chapter Eight

Risk versus Reward

"Follow your instincts. That is where true wisdom manifests itself."
-OPRAH WINFREY

Do not make the mistake of putting a price tag on your health or allowing someone else to—like a family member or an insurance company. You must answer a very important question. That is, "How much am I worth?" Many people fall into a trap that if someone else (insurance) is not paying for them to get pain relief or to be healthy then they will just learn to live with the problem and hope it gets better on its own. The fact is, health problems do not resolve on their own, they only get worse. It may be years before you see or feel the devastating results but you will. The worst attitude a person can have is of decided ignorance. An example would be that if you have to pay out of your own pocket you are not going to the doctor. That is an ignorant decision. Who ultimately gets hurt? Of course, you do! The vast majority of insurance companies pay for chiropractic care as they do medical care. But some insurance plans are better than others. Yours may be good today but in a year from now it can be completely different. Insurance does not pay for prevention of health problems nor do they pay for maintaining your health. That is why they do not pay for nutritional supplements at the health food store nor will they pay for your exercise program at the local fitness center. That is all up to you. You will derive great benefit by doing those things, but paying for them is your responsibility. Do not make a health decision based on your insurance company guidelines or by what doctor you can see or how much they will pay. Make a rational decision that will benefit you for your lifetime based on who can best treat your problem and improve your health. After all aren't you worth it? Don't you deserve the very best? Do highly paid entertainers, sports figures, and politicians deserve better health care than you do? No, of course not! But the reality is that when they want treatment for their health problems they seek out the very best health care professionals available. Their careers depend on them being healthy. They do not rely on what their insurance company allows. They can afford the care and they get it. Interestingly, these types of people understand the benefits of continued chiropractic care to keep themselves in the best possible health. People like Cher, Arnold Schwarzenegger, Tiger Woods, Denzel Washington, and Mel Gibson to name but a few because the list is too extensive. Because entertainers and professional athletes use Chiropractors does not mean it is expensive. In fact, it is very affordable for even the lower income families. It is the least expensive preventive and pain relief care in which a person can invest. You will spend less money on chiropractic care than you will spend on family vacations, entertainment, vehicle payments and maintenance. The question again is — are you worth it? Could you possibly invest in your own health as well as spending money on hair stylists, cosmetics, clothing, electronic toys, etc? The great thing about chiropractic is it will also make you feel better and give you the best performance to enjoy all those things you like to spend money on. An impressive aspect of the Pro-Adjuster is that the patient can see their progress unfold before their eyes. You will know with the doctor's help how your care is progressing so you will not need any more treatments than are absolutely necessary. You can save money or invest it. Remember you are in control of your health no one else. The people who best understand chiropractic receive it over their lifetimes to maintain their health and perform at a higher functional state. We do this as Chiropractors and so do our families. Dr. Laurel (Gretz) Pisciottano's father is Dr. Ronald J. Gretz, a Chiropractor. Dr. Laurel and her brother have received chiropractic treatments since they were born to keep them healthy. Dr. Laurel's brother is Dr. Jeffrey Gretz. He is a physician, and practices internal medicine. As adults they freely choose to receive chiropractic treatments as well as have their children treated. Do you think insurance pays for a lifetime of care? No, it is the choice of the individual and their complete understanding of how to keep the body as healthy as possible. What we are sharing with you as you read this book, are the inside secrets that all Chiropractors know and the how's and whys to keep their families healthy without dangerous drugs or needless surgeries.

On May 30, 1993, I got a second chance on a quality life. I had a kidney transplant at Presbyterian University Hospital in Pittsburgh, Pennsylvania. At first things were not going so well, my kidney didn't start functioning right away. My heart was also giving me problems. Things got a little better as my medications were adjusted. There were two medications that caused me problems that I could not deal with. They left me with a terrible stinging feeling in my hands and feet. After talking to Dr. Pisciottano, he thought he could help me. At that time he found a slight case of Arthritis in my neck. After several weeks of using the Pro-Adjuster, I definitely got relief. The problem in my neck also showed signs of improvements on my evaluation. As of now the tingling in my hands and feet are totally gone. I would definitely recommend Dr. Pisciottano and his staff for the caring and gentle treatment that I received.

- JOHN SHOMO

To achieve Peak Performance and improved health visit our website at www.pro-adjuster.com or call 1-877-942-4284.

Chapter Nine

Helping Another

"Do all the good you can, by all the means you can, in all the ways you can, in all the places you can, at all times you can, to all the people you can, as long as ever you can."

-John Westley

An all-encompassing feeling that runs through the fabric of our beings, something common to all humanity is the need to do something good for our fellow man. To leave something of our essence behind when we are gone. To leave sort of a footprint that marks our life showing we amounted to something and that our life was not in vain. Longfellow said, *"Times of great men all remind us, we can make our lives sublime, and departing leave behind us footprints on the sands of time."* This feeling or urge is hard to describe but seems to be encoded in our DNA.

Most doctors are especially aware of this and that is why we do what we do—we help humanity and bring people to a new level of health. Many people are also aware of this and continually strive to change life on this planet. Look at Gandhi, Mandela, and Mother Theresa to name a few. These people are the extremes and have sacrificed much in an effort to leave the world a better place than which they found it. There are also those who consistently involve themselves in worthwhile causes like charity organizations, feeding the hungry, and clothing and sheltering the poor. They do this to help, but also to satisfy that instinctive need to do good works for others. Many people do not have the opportunity on a regular basis to truly touch another person's life. They do not know how to better or improve a person's health or save a life. Most people live their lives creating their families, going to work, retiring and then leaving this world. Some never accomplish performing worthwhile selfless deeds for others nor fulfill that internal desire to change lives.

Perhaps you have had one or many opportunities to help another, but you haven't. We want you to know that the greatest feeling in the world is to change a life for the better, and you too can experience this feeling. It is not too late. You have the ability to do it over and over again. Regardless of your age, job, status or position in life you can change not just one life, but many. We are going to show you how and give you this opportunity. Don't be nervous. Your time has come to fulfill your own desire and need to help another. Once you do this and realize the true impact you have made on not only one life but many, because of all the people that person touches, you will want to do it again and again. Your involvement in improving one's health is much easier than you think. People all around you, your family, friends, co-workers, acquaintances and strangers you meet every day are suffering. They don't all suffer the same way and may not suffer all the time, but believe us they are in pain, and are looking for help but don't know where to turn for the right answers. This is proven by the huge industry that is pharmaceuticals and the billions of dollars spent by consumers every single day to handle their health problems. Let us tell you right now the drugs are not working and they are only feeding and perpetuating the health problems that we believe to be a global epidemic.

Over two million people yearly become toxically ill from properly prescribed medications and over 106,000 people die each year surrounding these circumstances. This is likely the fourth leading cause of death in the United States right behind cancer, heart attacks and strokes. We wouldn't want anyone in our families to die from drug complications. We wouldn't want it for our friends, acquaintances, and strangers on the street or for you! We don't believe you would want it for anyone you know either. That is why we have to find another way! We must all be alert to those around us and the signals they give us every day about their pain and suffering. We know you don't realize it is there but it is, you are simply not aware of the signals yet, although you will be. When you were a kid riding in your parents' car, you didn't pay any attention to where you were, what direction you were heading, your surroundings, or what color the traffic lights were. However, as you began your driving career you became acutely aware of those elements. It is now a part of your "driving life" to be aware of every traffic light, your surroundings, and any danger signal that may be a hazard to you and your passengers. You now are in tune with your driving environment. It is the same with people. You can become acutely aware to those around you, who may be giving signals that they are suffering.

Remember that these are the most common signals:
- Headaches
- Fatigue
- Sinus/Allergies
- Sleep Disturbances
- Mood swings (anxiety, depression)
- Pain in the body (especially the neck, shoulder area, upper and lower back)

Are there others? Of course there are. You just have to be aware and listen for the comments that people make in everyday ordinary conversations. But those listed are the most prevalent. They are also the most common indicators that a person's nervous system is being overloaded and shutting down. Over time the person will become increasingly ill with an array of problems that most doctors will have difficulty pinpointing and more trouble addressing the source of the problem. Those signals are also good indicators suggesting the need for chiropractic care. Those are the areas that chiropractic has some of the greatest and most profound affect on. Chiropractors routinely handle those conditions effectively and return people to a healthier lifestyle, free from the stress of persistent problem conditions. Those conditions that people often seem to believe they "just have to learn to live with". With the help of modern technology and advanced engineering, the Chiropractor with their unique skills and in depth understanding of human anatomy, and nervous system function, can use the Pro-Adjuster to accurately pinpoint problem areas and work to get an individual better, faster!

Your assignment then, if you choose to accept the challenge, is to better another human life and personally reap the benefits by enriching your own life in the process. You can impact the world and leave your mark behind. Simply start by changing one life. It is as easy as listening, caring and referring one person to a Chiropractor for a nervous system evaluation.

You should be fairly warned, however. If the person you refer goes to the Chiropractor and their life changes, your reward will be a great feeling of joy and success. You may become quite happy with the feeling you get when you do this, and continue to refer everyone you meet! Of course if you have not personally experienced chiropractic or chiropractic with the Pro-Adjuster, then the first life you need to change is your own.

I began treatment at Dr. Pisciottano's after being screened for Carpal Tunnel Syndrome. Because I was suffering from both pains in my left wrist and low back, I decided to take advantage of the opportunity and schedule an appointment for an evaluation. Before coming into the clinic, I tried physical therapy, which only helped temporarily. I wasn't satisfied with those results. I did not want to just live with the pain and give up doing the things I enjoy. Since treatment with the Pro-Adjuster, I can now do things that were impossible. I also sleep much better and can focus my attention on things more important than pain. I am very happy with the treatment that I received. I thank Dr. Pisciottano and his staff.

- FRANK WINTERS

Chapter Ten

Doctors and Their Patients Speak...

"There are just two ways of spreading light, to be the candle or mirror that reflects it."   -EDITH WHARTON

Although we are both experienced doctors who have collectively treated tens of thousands of people and administered hundreds of thousands of treatments with over 20 years of combined experience, our opinions do not speak as loudly as our patients or the patients of other doctors. You have now read accounts from a few doctors and their patients and we hope you have gained knowledge and understanding as to how to treat your body with the best treatment available. But to demonstrate the universality of our message we have included stories from more patients and doctors from around the globe. The power in these stories is incredible. They speak to the validity of chiropractic, the results and benefits with the Pro-Adjuster equipment, and the power of the body to heal naturally given the correct help. These patients have kindly volunteered to share their experiences in the hopes that they are able to help one person and save someone from pain. These people have nothing to gain but the satisfaction of knowing that their words will be a lasting and continuous testament to healing and a possible benefit to those that read it. We honor their courage to be a voice to you and others.

Let's allow the patients and their doctors to tell us more . . .

Peak Performance Health Care Center
Dr. Steve Arculeo
Chicago, Illinois

I remember the exact moment it happened. I was on my college tennis team, and one day when I was working out, I suddenly got a terrible pain in my neck and shoulder. That pain didn't go away. Over the next few weeks it got worse and worse. I could barely lift my arm over my head. The doctor I went to told me surgery was the only option. Then a friend of mine convinced me to give his doctor a try. That doctor did an exam, took some films, and then "adjusted" my spine. The adjustment didn't hurt; it actually felt good. After a couple of adjustments, I was out of pain and I had full use of my shoulder again! No drugs, no surgery — and my tennis game was better than ever. That new doctor was a chiropractor. I was so amazed by the results that I decided to go to chiropractic school myself. Now I am a chiropractic physician and people come to see me with their athletic injuries. They also come to me with their headaches, migraines, neck pain, back pain, knee pain, and other ailments. I have been fortunate to have had a very busy practice for the last twelve years. But I must say, our results were not always as dramatic as they tend to be now. The difference, which I believe is going to revolutionize care for the spine, is the Pro-Adjuster. Eight years ago, I studied with the late Dr. Vernon Pierce, one of the most famous and effective chiropractors of all time. At the research clinic at the Sherman College of Chiropractic, he introduced me to an early prototype of the Pro-Adjuster. I was astonished by the specificity of the diagnostic and spinal correction abilities of this computerized system. The Pro-Adjuster developed out of a combination of NASA engineering technology and Dr. Pierce's 30 years of clinical experience. But what impressed me the most was receiving an adjustment myself. I couldn't believe how good I felt afterward. Several years ago we started using the Pro-Adjuster at our center. We first tried it on our most difficult and severe cases, and we had huge breakthroughs with these patients. So we had to share this new technology with all our patients. The response was eye-opening. 95 percent of our patients chose the Pro-Adjuster over older manual chiropractic techniques. It was gentle — no twisting or popping of the spine — and the results were dramatic. They loved it! We had been very effective in the past at treating back pain and athletic injuries. Now, with the Pro-Adjuster, we were also seeing incredible results with headaches. Even patients deemed "incurable" by the most famous headache clinics in the country were seeing remarkable improvement at our center. Now we have become specialists in getting great results with all types of headaches.

One of my favorite headache-treatment successes was Diane.
Here's her story.

I've suffered with migraine headaches for 18 years. Six
months ago they became daily. I had tried everything. I'd been
to many migraine clinics here and in Canada. I tried beta-block-
ers, antidepressants, and was suggested to have shots of
Novocain injected into my neck. Ten years later nothing had
changed in the treatment of my headaches save the fact the
doctor put me on notice that the Imitrex I was taking could
cause a heart attack…nice thought. Several doctors told me the
migraines were just "my personality" and I should accept the
fact I would have them for the rest of my life. Perhaps it would
be worth mentioning that I compete nationally as a sculler and
I train six days per week, and I kept on this schedule right
through periods of intense migraines. One day I read about the
work being done at Peak Performance Health Center with Dr.
Arculeo and the Pro-Adjuster system. I read that he had great
results with world-class athletes, alleviating different conditions
including migraines. I went to the center and had the gamut of
tests and was evaluated with the Pro-Adjuster. Dr. Arculeo said
he found several problems in my neck and that I would be a
tough case, but he could help me. The rest is history. After only
a few months, I am 90 percent migraine free. I am feeling much
better overall; my body feels great, and my posture has also
improved. My training and competing is going great. Where I
mostly got silver metals last year, this year I got mostly gold. I
am so grateful to Dr. Arculeo and the Peak Performance Team.
I feel privileged to have found this clinic and this new technology. My wish is that more people can also benefit from the
Pro-Adjuster treatment.

DIANE ZIFF

Ruhland Chiropractic Clinic
Dr. Shaun R. Gifford
Bloomington, Minnesota

In 7th grade I had two severe accidents to my head. I hit my head on the ice, which required 75+ stitches and also a bike jumping accident, where I landed on my head. At age 12, I recovered from the injuries but it caught up to me in my junior year of high school. I took a hit to my head in a football game and within a week I was suffering with my first migraine.

I couldn't concentrate on my schoolwork, and it took me out of ball games, and I did not want to go out with friends. The pain was like a vice grip on the outside and a pressure gauge building up on the inside. I was sensitive to light and would get nauseous and need to lie down.

After a couple of months of treatment I realized my migraines were lessening. The past trauma to my head played a role in why I had the migraines. I realized that I did not have to live with them. My headaches were completely gone after six months.

It has been five years and have only had one migraine. As soon as I felt a headache coming on, I got adjusted with the Pro-Adjuster. It relieved a lot of the built up pressure in my head. I had less tension in the muscles that helped "hold" the adjustment. The Pro-Adjuster was a pain free adjustment that allowed me to relax while being adjusted. In less than two years, I have never fully developed a migraine.

The power that made the body certainly will heal the body. Chiropractic saved me from years of suffering. Because of my experience of being adjusted I became a doctor of chiropractic myself. Successfully treating thousands of people with the Pro-Adjuster.

The following is a success story by one of my patients, Susie.

I first came to Ruhland Chiropractic in September 2002 after being referred by a friend. I had tried everything else and seeing a chiropractor was my last resort for relief. I wasn't hesitant, I just wanted relief!

Being a flight attendant, I have had peripheral neuropathy in my feet since 1996 and I also have problems with my sciatic nerve on my right side due to pushing, pulling and lifting for my job for the last 29 years. I have tried numerous things to help with the pain in my feet including podiatrists, medical doctors, neurologists, and orthopedic doctors, having medication shots in the feet, physical therapy and ice.

I was getting very discouraged because nothing was working. I just wanted some relief from the pain. I was also beginning to think that I would have to live with this pain for the rest of my life! I couldn't do any activities such as play golf, go on vacation or anything that I enjoyed because it hurt to walk. I just did what I could and then suffered with the pain. The pain was excruciating, burning, and tingling in my feet. Standing and working was very difficult and the sciatic nerve pain was constant. It felt like I was 20 years older due to the pain that I was having.

Chiropractic and the Pro-Adjuster have helped me so much! It has helped the pain in my feet and also my sciatic nerve. I tell everyone about how chiropractic and the Pro-Adjuster have helped me!

I am now able to stand in place for longer periods of time, walk more and I just feel so much better in general. The benefits of my treatment have helped me so much. I tell everyone that they should try chiropractic because it can help them just like it helped me. I have realized that in the near future, I hope to be completely pain free!!! I also wanted to add that my clinic is great. Everyone there is so willing to help you. Thank you! Thank you! Thank you!

SUSIE C., FLIGHT ATTENDANT

Progressive Health Care Clinics
Dr. Matt Goldman
McMurray, Pennsylvania

When I was young, my father (who was an attorney) had the privilege of meeting a very dynamic Chiropractor by the name of Dr. Walter V. Pierce. My father was fortunate enough to not only to represent Dr. Pierce and his patients and help them legally, but he also became a very good friend with Dr. Pierce. In turn, Dr. Pierce introduced my father to several other chiropractors in our area.

As a result of my father's involvement in the field of chiropractic I grew up not only meeting and conversing with a lot of chiropractors, but I was also being treated by them and learning a lot about chiropractic and health. As I grew older and became more active in sports I began to become more interested in health and function of the human body. I began my interest with athletic training in high school and continued by learning as a sports science major at the University of Colorado. I graduated cum laud with a bachelor's degree in kinesiology and immediately enrolled in chiropractic school. I graduated from Life University with a Doctorate in Chiropractic and a Masters in Chiropractic Sports Sciences where I was actively involved in the care of the various athletes. Since 10th grade I have followed a very focused path that has lead me to where I am today, a doctor of chiropractic.

I have made it my mission to spread the word of chiropractic and get as many sick, hurt, and discouraged people better so that they are able to accomplish whatever goals they have set for themselves and most of all to be able to enjoy their life. One such person has been kind enough to share her story about our success in treating her with the Pro-Adjuster. Lisa DiGorio, a Café/Prep Server from South Park, PA, states,

My problems were those of lower back and neck pain. I had been suffering with them for over 15 years! I feel that it started after my first bad accident in 1986 when I had been hit from behind at 50 M.P. H. while I was at a dead stop. There were numerous accidents after this and with each accident the pain would come back a little more severe. I never went to any doctors, physical therapists or chiropractors for no other reason than other things seemed more important. Most of my relief came from a hydroculator that I would use from time to time or rarely some Tylenol. However, these were just temporary fixes and most of the time did not even help very much. It seemed it was just something that I was going to have to live with and as time went by it seemed to become part of my everyday life to live with pain. It was very frustrating! Everyday started with getting out of bed and saying my neck and low back hurt. The pain in my neck was always at its worst in the morning. I woke up very stiff and it was hard to move around. Sometimes when I would turn my head I would get a stabbing pinch. As for my low back the pain was constant and burning. Since being treated with the Pro-Adjuster my life has changed tremendously. I wake up every morning pain free and my flexibility and energy has greatly increased. The complaints like "my back is sore" and "my neck hurts" are gone from my vocabulary. The Pro-Adjuster is wonderful and Dr. Matt is an outstanding chiropractor. He took the time to listen and then using his expertise designed a program just for me. Needless to say this provided me with great results. Dr. Matt and his staff are very professional, friendly and helpful. It was and still is a pleasure to come to see him. I have nothing but compliments for him and would recommend his clinic to anyone. Thank you so much.

LISA DIGORIO, CAFÉ/PREP SERVER

Unlike most of the commercials you see on television, these results are typical! With the Pro-Adjuster I have personally successfully treated patients with ailments ranging from severe migraine headaches to digestive problems. With the Pro-Adjuster I have confidently treated 6 month old babies to 86 year old women. With the Pro-Adjuster I have happily treated patients with multiple sclerosis and multiple myeloma to help improve their quality and quantity of life. With the Pro-Adjuster I have become a better chiropractor and have been able to help people in ways that even surprise me sometimes!

Canonsburg Chiropractic Center
Dr. Laurel Gretz-Pisciottano
Canonsburg, Pennslyvania

As the child of a chiropractor, one could say that it was expected of me to become a chiropractor, to carry on the family business. This could not be further from the truth. My father, Dr. Ronald Gretz, has been an inspiration to me since I was very young. As a child, I heard him described as a doctor, a healer, a listener, a diagnoser, and a friend. He has helped thousands and thousands of people over the course of his 39 years as a chiropractor. I was one of his first patients. In 1965, as a recent Palmer graduate, my father left his pregnant wife in Iowa while he traveled to Pennsylvania looking for a home for his new family. Unexpectedly, their baby girl came two weeks early. I was born in Davenport, Iowa, the daughter of a 21-year-old first time mom, and a father that was out of town. There was a problem, however. I would not eat. Anything. At two weeks old, the doctors told my mother that I was literally starving. Medications were suggested and alternate feeding methods were tried, all without success. When my dad received the news, he immediately returned to Iowa to assess the situation. He found a problem and offered a different solution. He found that I had significant atlas misalignment, and proceeded to adjust me. To everyone's disbelief that had been involved with my case, this resolved the problem, and I began to eat as normally as any child. It was a beginning of a lifetime of chiropractic care. I never took medications, and did not have the need for a family doctor. If I got a sore throat, or the hiccups, or fell down, I asked for an adjustment. At the age of 12, I began to work in my father's successful chiropractic practice. I answered the phones and worked the front desk on Saturday mornings. I loved working at my first job. I began to notice that people came in cranky and in pain, and they left smiling. I began to observe the countless miracles that occurred every single day from the work of a chiropractor who really cared whether his patients got better. These miracles are the sole reason that I followed in my dad's footsteps. My purpose for this chosen career is to continue the work of the many chiropractors who pioneered our field, as well as to further advance our profession by utilizing the most updated and scientifically proven methods for chiropractic healthcare. Through this treatment, the subsequent results, and by educating the public on the many benefits of spinal and nervous system health, I will positively effect as many lives as possible. Maxine is one of my patients that benefited from chiropractic This is her story:

> I was diagnosed with fibromyalgia about ten years ago and have gone to more than ten specialists seeking relief from the terrible pain that I had been suffering with. After taking numerous prescriptions of anti-inflammatory medications, undergoing too numerous to count physical therapy trials, even massage therapy, with no results, I began to think there was no answer to this condition. Each time I would pursue another method of care, I would have high hopes, only to be let down again. I would experience a terrible burning sensation across both shoulders and both hips. My arms and legs ached so badly that I felt ten years older than I am. More than the pain, however, was the fact that I was no longer able to participate in family functions and activities. I would sometimes crawl instead of walking after a day's work in front of the computer. Everyone would tell me that I was no longer the "happy-go-lucky" person that I was. I was losing myself to pain. I began to feel depressed and agitated. This feeling was starting to take over, but I KNEW...somewhere, somehow, there was hope for me. Then the Lord led me to Canonsburg Chiropractic Center. I went there as a last resort. I have always believed in chiropractic, however, I thought it was for injured backs. I didn't think chiropractic could help me with my fibromyalgia. Boy was I ever wrong! After the first visit, I began to develop some confidence and that built as I started to improve. The pain-free treatment that I received with the Pro-Adjuster has absolutely changed my life. My impression of the Pro-Adjuster can be summed up with one word. AWESOME! My quality of living is vastly improved, because I have had such relief from the pain that I can once again participate in family activities. I can now lift and hold my grandchildren. My work days are pain free. I now have the long sought after answer to my fibromyalgia. I attribute my success to chiropractic, the understanding and compassion of my chiropractors, their staff, and the terrific results of the Pro-Adjuster.
>
> MAXINE BYSICK, HOSPITAL ACCOUNT REPRESENTATIVE

Dynamic Family Health Center
Dr. Jill Howe
Crystal Lake, Illinois

As an adolescent, I received a doctor's bag for Christmas containing a stethoscope, otoscope, a fake needle for giving shots, and sugar pills. I knew I wanted to be a doctor; however, in college I pursued Exercise Physiology. Finally, my mother convinced me that I could be a doctor with hard work and so, I pursued my childhood dream. Initially I wanted to become a cardiologist and perform life-saving surgeries. However, my real passion was to help people improve the quality of their lives before they required surgery and this is what chiropractic does. After ten years in practice, I learned about the Pro-Adjuster. At first I couldn't see its value since I was achieving great results without it. However, I had an opportunity to experience first hand what it could do when I injured my back horseback riding and several doctors worked on me, but I had no lasting improvement. My first treatment with the Pro-Adjuster left me 100% pain-free immediately! I knew at once I had to have this technology for my patients. All of our results have been phenomenal! One patient who presented with a very debilitated condition — couldn't walk without a walker, couldn't drive and had daily headaches, diabetes and high blood pressure — now drives himself to his appointments and walks unassisted. Following two months of care his internal medicine physician and his neurologist noticed that all his lab results were normalizing and advised him to "continue whatever he was doing". He had seen nine other doctors (without success) who sentenced him to his debilitated life forever. Following our care he exclaimed, "Thank you for giving me my life back!" The Pro-Adjuster has not only revolutionized my practice, but also my life as I leave at the end of the day with more energy and less wear and tear on my body. This technology has increased my certainty that I am achieving the best results possible for my patients. My purpose as a doctor is foremost to educate my patients regarding the function of their bodies so they can understand how their health problem developed. My mission is to provide the highest quality health care possible to keep my patients from unnecessary surgeries and drugs and to refer them to the proper specialist if I am unable to assist them. One of my patients expressed his satisfaction with the Pro-Adjuster as follows:

Far too long I used to fear sleeping for more than 5 hours. Because of my schedule working on-air early in the morning, Monday through Friday, I'd sleep just enough to function during the day. Seemed every weekend that I got more than 5 hours sleep, I couldn't lift myself off my bed without discomfort and considerable effort. I knew I couldn't continue like this, but I didn't think the medical community could really help, other than to offer muscle relaxant type medicine. Then as I began an hour show called "Stew's News and Views", I hooked up with Dr's. Jill Howe and Jason Hui for their daily segment. We discussed a myriad of conditions and how they helped people. I grew curious as they described patient success with the Pro-Adjuster. We scheduled a visit and I came over for a discussion on how I was physically doing. I had had more need for the Pro-Adjuster than I initially realized. Dr. Howe described how my spine was so out-of-line. I was a definite candidate for not only adjustments, but physical therapy. At the end of the session, which I experienced as painless, I got in my car and felt as though I could adequately straighten up without feeling discomfort. Sure the discomfort returned, but I had started a road to feeling better. The doctors also noted I was losing my voice too often. As a broadcaster, losing one's voice makes it much harder to do anything on-air. Dr. Howe felt she could help in this regard by doing spinal realigning in my neck area with the Pro-Adjuster. So far, I've not lost my voice, and that's like a miracle. I had lost my voice three times before I started chiropractic, once for a week. During this time, I began feeling better, I referred my sons. My youngest is suffering from asthma and my oldest has chronic enlarged lymph nodes. They've been doing the Pro-Adjuster and physical therapy. My oldest has improved his range of motion in his neck. I'm not completely sure on how my youngest has improved from his asthma but I do know he hasn't been sick or require his asthma inhaler as often. Thanks Dr's. Howe and Hui, and your great staff. You've worked hard giving my family a renewed energy and discomfort-free outlook on life.

STEW COHEN, NEWS DIRECTOR
STAR 105.5 AND WAIT

Montgomery Chiropractic
Dr. Rebecca Ulsh Kloczkowski
Cincinnati, Ohio

Growing up in Springfield, Ohio was basically uneventful until I was 10 years old. That year, my father was stricken with severe pain in his right abdomen and shoulder causing lots of family concern. After visiting medical doctors, he was told that his gall bladder was diseased and had to be removed as soon as possible. As the family prepared for the inevitable surgery, Dad's brother-in-law, Harold, visited to talk about the operation. "Jack, do you want to go under the knife?" Harold questioned my father. Then he added "If I were you, I would go to a Chiropractor. A pinched nerve in your back can cause organ problems in the same way it can cause muscle pain." My Dad responded "I didn't know that. Maybe I should see one." Skeptical and as a last resort, he went to a Chiropractor who discovered a T-4 nerve impingement. After adjustments and diet recommendations, my father was cured and never had a relapse. The episode made a lasting impression on me, because the Chiropractor saved my father from surgery. A few years later, when I also benefited from Chiropractic care, I decided to become a Doctor of Chiropractic. My eagerness to learn this skill and to help others motivated me to complete my degree at Palmer College in record time. I finished as one of the youngest graduates and achieved the highest honors. After establishing a practice in northern Cincinnati, Ohio, the past 20 years has been dedicating to serving the community. Whether treating the elderly or infants and every age in between, my practice is devoted to healing, and then assisting my patients in achieving a holistic approach to health and living. As a Born Again Christian, I see how Chiropractic is a biblical solution to medical problems, namely, it helps the body heal itself with its God-given gifts. After many years in practice and many hours of continuing education, I have learned that Chiropractic care continues to advance with new techniques and technology. Hence, the purpose of my practice, Montgomery Chiropractic and Wellness Center, is to provide our patients the highest quality care, treatments and products as well as providing the leading edge technology to achieve maximum health and wellness. For example, the Pro-Adjuster and it revolutionary results epitomizes our commitment to our patients and their well being. The following story highlights the benefits of Chiropractic and the capabilities of the Pro-Adjuster. One of my patients would like to share his experiences in the hopes that others will discover its benefits.

My life has always been an active one reflecting the adage "Work hard and play hard." As a Vice President of Sales and Marketing, there is never a dull moment at work. At play pursuing a variety of activities such as skiing, scuba diving, biking, skydiving and other sports, there is always the potential for injury. About 10 years ago, I experienced a potentially life changing injury. While biking with friends, I was thrown from my bike and hit the pavement head first. When I regained consciousness, my hands and arms were paralyzed for several minutes. Medics responded and I was strapped to a board for x-rays and tests. The diagnosis involved a severe compression of the C-5/C-6 disk that would require vertebra fusion as soon as possible. Under hospital observation for 5 days, I was finally discharged with instructions to return in 30 days for the operation. Determined to avoid the surgery, I returned to the gym for very light weight training and stretching exercises in the pool. Though I considered Chiropractors as "quacks", I sought the care of one. Gradually, my condition improved to the point that my medical doctor decided to postpone surgery for several months. My training eventually returned to my pre-injury levels, and with the help of my Chiropractor, my condition no longer required surgery. My Chiropractor had performed a miracle! Ten years later, I continue to lift weights and enjoy a variety of sports activities. Sometimes, I suffer from stiffness, pain and some cracking sensations in my neck after vigorous exercise. Needless to say, regular Chiropractic care is a "must" for my cervical condition as well as my overall health. Recently, my wife, Dr. Rebecca Kloczkowski, began treating me with her new instrument, the Pro-Adjuster. The results have been outstanding. My chronic pain has been eliminated, and I enjoy excellent neck flexibility. Finally, the cracking sensations in my neck have disappeared. Yes, I married my Chiropractor that saved me from surgery. Her "Chiropractic Touch" has kept me physically healthy ever since my accident, but now with the Pro-Adjuster, she has helped me reach a new level of wellness. Thank you, Honey, and thank you, Pro-Adjuster.

BOB KLOCZKOWSKI

Progressive Health Care Clinics
Dr. Kevin Laster
McMurray, PA

Since a very young age I have experienced the benefits of chiropractic care firsthand. When I was born I was fortunate to have a cousin who was a Chiropractor. I am confident that chiropractic has made a difference, providing me with good health my entire life. My experience has had such a strong impact that I decided to become a chiropractor to help others become healthy through natural means. Even as a teenager I could see that the medical model was to give drugs. But this approach didn't fix the problem. Through chiropractic I have found the solution to many health problems that people experience. I am happy to share my story and that of a patient's with you..

In the summer of 2002, I began experiencing excruciating pain in my lower back and leg. This all came on suddenly and it seemed without any cause. The pain was so bad that I couldn't go to work or more importantly continue to train horses.

Just as sudden as the pain began, it ended. I thought I was in the clear. In November of 2002, I suffered another bout with the pain. I could no longer deal with it. My back and leg were affecting my every day life too much.

The first thing I did was visit my physician. He prescribed steroids. That treatment didn't really help at all. The next step I took was to visit a chiropractor. The manual manipulation worked for a short time but didn't seem to last. I finally went to have an MRI done. The only other option I thought available to me was surgery.

A young woman who came into the post office where I work mentioned that she thought I should try Progressive Health Care Clinics. I decided to take her advice. I actually came in looking for some quick relief. Well, I got the quick relief and more.

I now feel eighty percent better and surgery is no longer a route that I consider. I am glad that Progressive Health Care Clinics found me.

RANDY HAMILTON, POSTAL WORKER

Chiropractic Center of Virginia Beach
Dr. James Maggio
Virginia Beach, Virginia

At this time I feel privileged to share my chiropractic story with you. I began having an interest in chiropractic because of my very successful personal experience. In my late teens I had injured my shoulder lifting at work. A few weeks later I was unable to lift my arm over my head. I went to see my friend's chiropractor and within three treatments my shoulder was fine! I thought that was good but what occurred next really blew my mind. I was suffering with allergies, asthma, and every year I got strep throat. I was always sick with colds and flus. My allergies were so bad I couldn't walk into a house where a cat lived even if it was outside. I had asthma attacks three or four times a week in the middle of the night. I had been on medications practically my whole life. All of this cleared up with chiropractic treatments!!! What a great surprise and a wonderful difference this made in my life. That started my snowballing interest in chiropractic.

At first I told everyone with allergies and asthma to go see a chiropractor. Some did and some improved. The gratitude they shared with me about their improvement was so overwhelming that I decided it was time for me to help others too. So I picked up my belongings and headed out to chiropractic college. My years in practice have been remarkable. People from all walks of life with all kinds of ailments from allergies to ulcers and all kinds of problems in between are getting better with chiropractic care. It is remarkable!!! So my purpose started out to help allergy sufferers, now it is to help those who want help no matter what the problem. I don't run a 100% success rate, but it is really close. The Pro-Adjuster makes our diagnosis and treatment tremendously easier and much more efficient.

One of my patients wanted to share her story of success with you. We hope her story will help give you or a loved one hope for similar success.

In 1959 I was on my way to drop my mother in law off at home. We were waiting for a long line of cars to go by so we could make a left turn. Out of nowhere a car slammed into the back of us, going forty miles per hour. Our car flew forward about half a block, and the rear impact forced the back seat forward. It pinned me up against the steering wheel. I was so worried about my mother I didn't think about being hurt, or going to the hospital. The next day I couldn't get out of bed!

When I went to my doctor he took x-rays, gave me medications, and painkillers, and had me wear a body and neck brace for six months. I put up with the pain from my neck to my feet. When I was stressed my sciatic burned if I moved. I had stiffness in my low back and numbness in my shoulders that hurt me to drive. I had acid reflux and bad bouts with sinuses. I used to dance, exercise, and walk four miles a day, but I had to stop. Two years after the accident my daughter was born. It was difficult to take care of her. I had a nanny come help me with the kids seven years. She helped with the heavy work and cleaning. I used to do receptions, retreats, and such for the church. After being on my feet for a period of time, my back was in excruciating pain. I am now a certified spiritual director and chaplain at the Bon Secour Maryview Hospital. The rheumatologist gave me many shots in my knees and shoulder joints; they said they couldn't give me anymore. Two series of physical therapy helped, but the pain would come back. The orthopedic surgeon said surgery was the only way because therapy and shots didn't work. My internist friend advised me not to have surgery because most likely I would have to have more surgery. One morning in October 2001 I woke up, again I couldn't move! My daughter called, I told her I couldn't get out of bed. She called our friend, a very respected pediatrician, Dr. Linda Rodriguez. She came over and told me about Dr. Maggio. She wanted me to go, but I said "NO WAY" I don't believe in those "quack" chiropractors! Although, if Dr. Rodriguez goes it must be all right. Treatments began immediately with the Pro-Adjuster. Soon my acid reflux got better. I am not on heavy doses of sinus medications, and in January 2002 I was off my back pain medications I have been taking for 45 years which resulted in bleeding ulcers. On a normal day I can stand for long periods of time and my back hardly hurts. My chiropractic healing has been great physically and mentally! The Pro-Adjuster was such a relief! I am so happy that I can be a strong inspiration for others to overcome pain and obstacles. Thanks Dr. Maggio and staff.

MARJORIE CURTIS
BOARD CERTIFIED HOSPITAL CHAPLAIN

Back to Action Chiropractic
Dr. Sam Nia, Cumming, Georgia

As a pre-med student I had a strong interest in helping people and thought my life was right on track. Then one day my father was checked into the hospital for complications from bronchitis. I later learned that he had damaged arteries in his heart and would need open heart surgery. But first he would have to perform a stress test (running on a treadmill and measuring heart function). I finally arrived home on Christmas break to visit and his testing was scheduled on the day before Christmas Eve. We all felt helpless, because there was no other option and the surgery would have to take place once the test was complete. On the day of my father's test, I was home with my brother waiting to hear from my mother. The next thing I know, my mother arrives home, but with company. My friend and his mother had to drive her home because she was upset and would not let her drive. At this point I knew something had gone wrong. Apparently, while undergoing the test, my father collapsed on the treadmill and died from heart failure, in the presence of three cardiologists. This was the day my whole life changed. According to the doctors, my father's heart had extensive damage due to prescription medications taken for over 17 years for his ulcerative colitis. He didn't have a previous heart condition! After this experience, I had to really think whether medicine was going to be my future. That's when I discovered that chiropractic was the fastest growing alternative healthcare profession. I decided to do some research and saw how phenomenal chiropractic really is. I decided to complete my pre-med studies and then transfer to a chiropractic school to start my new journey. Discovering my purpose was still the same, but instead of promoting drugs or surgery, I could help people using a non-drug alternative approach to health. Further, my journey took me across the world on a mission trip to Chisinau, Moldova. We delivered chiropractic care to approximately 40,000 people. They suffered from a wide variety of painful musculoskeletal and neurological conditions. These people did not have a variety of healthcare options due to their economically challenged country. The trip was truly phenomenal. As each day went by, I witnessed more chiropractic results and miracles. I realized my chiropractic journey would prove to be a life changing profession, not only for me, but also for my patients. Now as a chiropractor, I am able to improve the health and wellbeing of patients every day, including Donald who has improved with the Pro-Adjuster.

While returning to my girlfriend's apartment from the North Carolina Mountains, I lost control of the car, and went off a cliff. As the car flew towards the river, I was thrown 50 yards down, landing on rocks. Although I suffered a fractured neck, bruised spinal cord and a broken left elbow, I was able to find my way back up to the top. I was transported by helicopter to the Womack Military Hospital where a "halo" was placed on me. I had a C1 and C2 fusion done at 4 months. I wore this "halo" for a total of 8 long months. Finally the day came for it to be removed. I remember it was one of the happiest days in my life. Once removed, a Philadelphia Collar was given to me to wear for 7 to 8 months. As I left the Military Hospital nothing was ever said about my rehabilitation. No one had prepared me for what was in my future. My upper body muscles were weak from wearing the "halo". My neck, back and shoulder muscles spasmed continuously. I began to have stabbing pains in the back of my neck as well as headaches, which eventually turned into migraines. I had no idea what to do or what type of doctor I should see. Over the next 14 years I received treatments from physical and massage therapists, traditional chiropractic adjustments and pain management doctors (radio frequency treatments). I even went to neurologists over the years to be treated for migraine headaches. Nothing I tried would eliminate my pain and suffering for more than a week or two. I began to think that the pain was going to be part of my life forever. Fortunately for me, the company I worked for had a mandatory ergonomic workshop for the employees. A young lady named Ingrid was doing the presentation. At one point she passed out a questionnaire concerning the condition I was in at the time. The next day I received a call and was offered a free consultation. Soon Dr. Nia was regularly treating me using soft touch adjustments. My neck is more straight than curvy. My first visit took care of the muscle pain that I had in my right shoulder for 14 years. It was remarkable! I finally found a doctor who was interested in treating my condition and not my symptoms. Now my muscle spasms are a rare occurrence. I have no more migraine headaches, the pain in my neck, back and shoulders have been decreased greatly. I am now being treated with the Pro-Adjuster and am determined to get the curve back in my neck. I am confident that in Dr. Nia's care this will become reality very soon. Thank you, Dr. Nia, for giving me my life back.

DONALD H. RICE III, SUBSTITUTE TEACHER

Dr. Peter G. Phillips
Vancouver, Washington

In 1982 as a senior in high school, I suffered a major knee injury while playing football. I was taken to the local hospital where I was told I would need knee surgery. In searching for any alternatives, my parents took me to an osteopath. He was probably 70 years old. He played around with my knee until it "cracked". He said maybe you won't need that surgery after all, come back and see me in a week. I did return in a week, and unfortunately I was told that I would need surgery.

I could not help but think of the potential power of this cracking of my knee to possibly avoid surgery, what was it, how could it work? I spoke with the Osteopath about his profession. It was quite enlightening I learned the real path to wellness, "The body's innate or inborn ability to heal itself". He did not recommend that I pursue osteopathy. He said that Osteopaths have changed over the years, and only think medically. They no longer think about the bodies own ability to heal itself. He said if you really want to change the lives of people and are considering a profession in health care, that I should research a career in Chiropractic. "Chiropractors have remained loyal to their roots, and help millions of people get well naturally". I couldn't help but to be moved to look at Chiropractic as a profession.

I decided to spend some time with a local Chiropractor to see if this was possibly the profession for me. I always knew that I wanted to be in a profession that would allow me to help people. I had a great experience following this Chiropractor around while he was treating patients in his office. I was absolutely amazed at how much his patients appreciated him.

He seemed to always have loaves of bread or plates of cookies on his counter brought in from appreciative patients. I knew at that time I wanted to help people the same way he was. I am very thankful to serve the people of my community, as their Chiropractor. I cannot imagine a better way to help sick people get well.

My daughter and I are both avid believers in chiropractic care. We have used a chiropractor both for health maintenance and in times of a specific physical need. Chiropractic care became ever so necessary when my grandson was born. Due to some physical difficulties with my daughter, it was necessary for her to be induced in week 35. When my grandson was born, we knew right away, there were problems as he was having difficulty breathing. Tyler was diagnosed with a neumo-tho-rax. After a 10 day stay in the Neonatal Intensive Care Unit, he was released. Within four days of coming home, he started to have seizures and was rushed back to the hospital where he spent another 10 days.

After his discharge, I made a visit to Dr. Peter Phillips for an adjustment. I discussed with him the situation with my grandson Tyler. Dr. Phillips shared with me the latest information he had learned regarding infants and because of the trauma of the birthing process the benefits of having the baby adjusted. We knew there was a window of time to begin that process for the results to be most effective.

We brought Tyler in and began regular adjustments. I am so excited to share that Tyler did not have another seizure. Another benefit was when he started to have a little colic, with regular adjustments, it never became a problem.

There is not doubt because Dr. Peter Phillips is committed to continually updating and educating himself on the latest technology that today Tyler is a happy, healthy and very smart little boy. (Just ask his grandma).

I have been so thrilled by the results Tyler has had with the Pro-Adjuster that I am telling everyone about it. Dr. Peter Phillips compassion and commitment to his patients makes him stand out above the rest. Thank you Dr. Phillips!

BARBARA LIPNOS

Progressive Health Care Clinics
Dr. Geno A. Pisciottano
McMurray, Pennsylvania

As a child, I never went to see a medical doctor when I was sick. Instead, I went to Dr. Walter Vernon Pierce, a chiropractor in my hometown. I would visit Dr. Pierce when I was hurt, had a cold or just did not feel well. I never had the experience of going through the medical route of care with medication and/or surgery. From the very beginning of my life, I was under the influence of chiropractic care.

The time for college came and my main concern was to choose a profession where I could help people. I did my undergraduate work in a field that was non-related to chiropractic, but I always contemplated becoming a chiropractor. Even the courses that I took during my undergraduate study included several scientific-based classes because I could not get the idea of becoming a chiropractor out of my mind. I graduated and obtained a job in my field of study, but quickly realized that I was not helping people all the time. Sometimes my actions would hurt individuals as much as help them. I knew I needed to find a career that only helped people with no downside to the job.

I decided to go back to school to become a chiropractor and fulfill the dream that had always been in my heart and in the back of my mind. I chose Palmer College of Chiropractic and graduated in 1996. I then joined forces with my brother, who was already a practicing chiropractor.

After practicing chiropractic for several years, I realized that I was indeed helping many people. Unfortunately, numerous people still needed care, but were hesitant to try chiropractic. The introduction of the Pro-Adjuster opened the door to many patients that would not have considered chiropractic in the past. Now, I am helping people that previously may have chosen another type of care. Their alternative to chiropractic may have put them through years of physical therapy and possibly even surgery. I hear from individuals on a daily basis that wish they would have sought chiropractic sooner but they were afraid of being manually adjusted. The Pro-Adjuster eliminates that fear and helps people regain their well being. Today, I never regret my choice of profession. Chiropractic helps me reach my number one goal in life, to help people. Achieving that goal on a daily basis is easy with the Pro-Adjuster. Chiropractic and the Pro-Adjuster is a natural combination to helping the human race. Being a Pro-Doctor is always exciting and worthwhile, just ask my patients.

Before I came to Progressive Healthcare I was having excruciating neck and left arm pain. I also had numbness in my fingers and shooting pains into my fingers. I was diagnosed with a bulging disc in my neck and my doctor wanted to perform surgery. I did not want to have surgery. The pain was so bad I couldn't sleep, I couldn't play with my kids, and I had pain 24 hours per day. I was taking Vioxx, Ibuprofen, and was wearing a neck collar. I could barely hold my head up. I hadn't been able to work for two months.

My brother in law referred me to Progressive Healthcare and Dr. Pisciottano. I had never been to a chiropractor and I was very doubtful that the adjustments would help, but after a few treatments I started feeling some relief. I have had great success with the Pro-Adjuster treatments and therapy. I was able to return to work, and continue with my hunting and fishing hobbies. I have actually had 100% improvement in the functioning of my neck and arm and subsequently have referred my family and friends in for treatment. I just came back in for treatment after a two week withdrawal period and I am still feeling great. I plan to continue with Wellness Care. I am so grateful to Dr. Pisciottano and the Pro-Adjuster.

MIKE SUSKO

Porreca Chiropractic Center, Inc.
Dr . Joseph Porreca
Belle Vernon, Pennsylvania

I've wanted to become a chiropractor since the 8th grade. I can remember my next door neighbor visiting the chiropractor, not just for back pain but for relief of symptoms related to the common cold and other problems that I never knew could be helped without the use of drugs or surgery. My interest in chiropractic was heightened when reading articles in various muscle magazines. I was in junior high school at the time and involved in wrestling and would read those magazines for weight training advice. Often times these magazines would have articles in them pertaining to health and the care of various training injuries, many times the articles were authored by chiropractors thus my interest in chiropractic grew even more. Now, that I am a doctor of chiropractic I take great pleasure in knowing that I have the opportunity to help the people of my community live a more comfortable and healthier life. My purpose as a chiropractor is to always be a positive force in my community and to help as many people as we possibly can. The results I've seen in chiropractic since beginning to utilize the Pro-Adjuster in my practice have been nothing short of astounding. Patients have informed me that they've benefited by getting relief of various ailments from neck and lower back pain to asthma, prostate problems and swelling in the lower legs.

Realizing that the brain controls all of the organs of the body and thus all of the bodily functions. Also, understanding that the brain communicates with the body via the spinal cord and peripheral nerves. It is my personal mission in chiropractic to keep the nervous system free from interference that can be caused by subluxations. In summary, my mission as a chiropractor is to detect and correct vertebral subluxations in order that the nerves can be free of interference. When the nervous system is free of interference it can function to 100% of its capacity thus allowing the body to function at 100% of its potential.

Now, allow me to introduce one of my patients to you. Her name is Susan Ritsko and this is the story of her success from chiropractic treatment with the Pro-Adjuster.

I first came to Dr. Porreca on December 11, 2002, I was suffering from extreme headaches that had started 15 years ago. At the time I thought they were sinus or allergy related. I had tried everything from using a heating pad to taking Tylenol and ibuprofen to Claritin, Allegra, Nasonex and Flonase, but the pain did not stop and I was left with an upset stomach and developed a tolerance to the medication. When the headaches were at their worst (sometimes lasting 2 weeks) I would get so nauseated and had to nap all the time just to get rid of them. I became easily agitated, depressed and sometimes even too tired and sick to go to work. I had lost the zest for life as if I was an 80-year-old woman. The medications no longer worked. I felt that there was no answer or help for these headaches and felt I would have to live with the pain for the rest of my life.

I had read on the Internet and through relatives that headaches could be relieved through chiropractic care. That is when Dr. Porreca came into my life. After only a couple treatments on the Pro-Adjuster my headaches were less severe and now they are a thing of the past. One of the best benefits of my treatment with the Pro-Adjuster was realizing that I no longer had agonizing headaches or mood swings and would recommend the Pro-Adjuster to anyone. It's great! I have a much better outlook on life and more energy. Things that I thought I had lost forever. Thanks Doc!

SUSAN RITSKO, SECRETARY

Fullerton Chiropractic Wellness Center
Dr. Michele E. Quam
Fullerton, California

During the delivery of my second child I experienced extreme low back pain and the contractions went across my back instead of my abdomen. After delivering Charity, a beautiful little girl, I found that I had trouble just doing the simple tasks of normal daily activities. Just a few days after I got home from the hospital I received an ad/coupon in the mail for a chiropractic examination and consultation. So I called and made my first chiropractic appointment. After the exam and x-rays he told me that I needed treatment to correct the misalignment in my low back and he adjusted me the old fashioned way, by putting me on my side, bending my leg up and putting a lot of pressure on my low back. It worked, I got better and the pain was gone in just a few visits. It was my first adjustment and that was over 30 years ago. At the time I worked for the phone company in a nontraditional job that required climbing ladders and pulling cable, so over the years I depended on Dr. Jeff Lowy for a lot of adjustments, because my back was never the same after delivering my second child. Over the many years of seeing Dr. Jeff he would always tell me that we needed more chiropractors and that I should go back to school, etc. Well, I had those velvet handcuffs on and by now I was in management (15 years later) and making a good living, but felt dissatisfied and unchallenged in what I was doing. Then I got lucky and the phone company broke up (divestiture) and they were offering early retirement incentives, so I happily volunteered and took them up on the offer. I went back to school to get my undergrad credits, entered Chiropractic College in 1989 and graduated with honors in 1992. I am thankful for Dr. Jeff Lowy's encouragement and direction. Now I have the opportunity to help others as he had once helped me.

In January 2003 I was at a seminar in Las Vegas and met Dr. Pisciottano and his amazing machine. He adjusted me only once at the seminar and it was by far the best adjustment I had ever had and I have had many. Believe me when you have a bad back for 30 years and have only been helped by chiropractic you have had a lot of adjustments. When I got home to California I decided to purchase a Pro-Adjuster for my patients, so that I could help them feel their very best and experience the proven results that only a Pro-Adjuster adjustment can administer. Dr. Pisciottano has put chiropractic on a whole new level and the world owes him a tremendous thank you. Thank you Dr. Pisciottano.

I would like to introduce my patient Wendy Carter and let her share her chiropractic experience and awesome results that she has recently obtained. After months of manual (old-fashioned adjustments) she had improved, but had reached a plateau and still suffered from chronic pain. After just a few adjustments with the Pro-Adjuster she improved dramatically.

A mutual friend recommended me to Dr. Quam in the summer of 1999 when I complained of neck and back pain after a Tae Kwon Do tournament. Shortly thereafter, I was involved in a serious auto accident that left me with severe neck and shoulder pain. I was unable to continue the practice of Tae Kwon Do and worse yet, I could not play golf. The pain had a dramatic negative impact on my day to day activities as well as my state of mind. After several months of intensive chiropractic treatment and physical therapy, my pain subsided to the point that I was able to resume playing golf. Although I continued to experience neck and shoulder pain it was not as severe or as debilitating. In February 2003, Dr. Quam added a new piece of equipment to her practice called the Pro-Adjuster. Dr. Quam explained how the Pro-Adjuster worked, that it was safer and more consistent than a traditional adjustment, and that it provided objective feedback as to the effectiveness of the adjustment. I was skeptical, but consented to a Pro-Adjuster treatment. I was amazed at how fast and easy the treatment was. The before and after graphs showed where my problem areas were and how the treatment helped those areas. After just four Pro-Adjuster treatments, I am virtually pain free. I'm 42 years old and I feel like I'm 25. My golf game is better, my attitude is better and my life is better.

WENDY CARTER, BUSINESS OWNER

ADIO Chiropractic Center
Dr. Donald F. Riefer
Cedartown, Georgia

I had an automobile accident in Houston, TX in 1993. I was told that the loss of motion, stiffness and pain could only be managed by pain medication. Thinking about this and knowing that there weren't any broken bones I told a friend about it and he recommended that I see a chiropractor. Up until this point I didn't know what a chiropractor was let alone that they even existed. This is one of the best-kept secrets in health care. Well to make a long story short in 3 weeks I had full range of motion and in 3 months time I was running 5-minute miles again at age 36. I was impressed. This was my first chiropractic experience. Why did I change careers when I was working in the computer industry and making a great living you ask? I was taking a yoga and meditation seminar in upstate New York. On my arrival the first person I met was a chiropractor which I thought nothing of. Throughout the weeklong stay it seemed that everyone that I met was either a chiropractor or in school to be a chiropractor. After the 7th day and meeting another chiropractor I stopped and asked myself what is up with meeting all of these chiropractors? Do I need an adjustment or something? Well it was time to depart and those of us leaving had a chance to say bye to the meditation instructor. As I began to sit one of the monks asked me if I had a question to ask Swami Chidvilasanda and a voice from within me spoke out and said yes. I was totally surprised that a response came from me since I didn't have a pre-meditated question. The Swami said great and instructed me to sit next to him. While I was sitting and waiting for my turn to say bye, the Swami asked me what was the question that I had. Once again that voice spoke out from within me and said that I wanted to ask Swami Chidvilasanda for her blessings to go back to school to become a chiropractor. The Swami looked at me and said great, that is a noble question. I didn't have a pre-meditated question once again. When it was my turn to speak to Swami Chidvilasanda and asked her about going back to school to become a chiropractor she nodded and gave me her approval. As I got up to leave I heard that voice inside of me say AHHH you finally got it!

Monday morning I went to my office and found the catalog to the local college open to Biology 101. I asked everyone in my office "who put the catalog on my desk" and no one admitted to it. Well, at this point I thought about humoring myself. I called Life College and asked them what it would take for me to attend their chiropractic school;

they faxed the information back to me immediately. I contacted all of the schools that I have attended over the years and had a reply from Life College within 2 days. Interestingly enough one of the courses I needed to take was the Biology 101. The semester had already begun but I decided to call the college and asked them about the course, they said that there was one seat left in that class. From that point on I started taking the pre-requisites. Two weeks into the course the company I was working for was sold and all of our jobs were gone. Lucky for me, I was the programmer that they needed to do a conversion for them and it gave me enough money to pay for all of my pre-requisites, pay all of my living expenses and make the trip to Life College. That is why I am a chiropractor today!

After being in a car wreck, my neck, head, and back was hurting for two months. Before the car wreck I had been having headaches for several years. To try to help my pain, I took Aleve, Tylenol, Tylenol III, ibuprofen, Percoset, Darvacet, and Maxalt. Nothing was working. After several hours or if I was lucky, the next day, the pain would return. I became irritable because I felt nothing could ever help me. But the one realization that I have had was that I didn't know my problem was that bad because I was getting use to it. When the pain was at its worst, I would have to lay down for not hours but days at a time. I was hardly around my friends or family due to the amount of time I was ill or asleep. I just knew I could not have a normal life. This is when Dr. Riefer came into my life. One of my teachers is his patient and I heard her say how much better he made her feel. I knew it was worth taking a chance since nothing else was working. After one month of treatment with the Pro-Adjuster, I am able to do more and I don't have a headache everyday. I can even baby sit now because I am not so ill. Now I know that a normal life is possible for someone like me too.

AMANDA BECK, HIGH SCHOOL STUDENT

Silva Family Chiropractic
Dr. John L. Silva
Port St. Lucie, Florida

I will never forget my first experience with chiropractic. I was nineteen years old and had injured my low back while working on a construction site. The pain was a severe stabbing pain that radiated down both legs. At the time of the injury I was frightened. For at least thirty minutes I couldn't even force myself to stand up. I really thought I was paralyzed. After three days in bed, a friend recommended I go to a chiropractor for some relief. I had no idea what a chiropractor did or what chiropractic was all about. I felt there was no other choice. Needless to say it worked, within three visits I was getting some relief and I learned what chiropractic was all about. Armed with this new knowledge I continued my care to maintain my spine to avoid future problems.

The benefits of chiropractic didn't stop with my low back injury. Under regular chiropractic care I was also able to overcome allergies that had plagued me since childhood for which my medical doctor had me on daily medication. I am happy to say that I am no longer dependant on the medication and live life allergy free. It was evident to me throughout the years of living a chiropractic lifestyle that the body, when given the chance, has the ability to heal naturally. It was with this realization that I decided to become a doctor of chiropractic. I am now able to share with others what I was fortunate enough to discover — the gift of chiropractic healing.

My purpose is to serve the sick, injured and those who wish to take their health to a whole new level. I strive daily to inform my patients and every one I meet that chiropractic care not only helps people with their pain and health problems but more importantly allow individuals to reach their full human potential. It is through the nervous system that life is expressed and when the nervous system is functioning properly and to its fullest, true health can be attained. My mission as a chiropractor is to make a difference in the lives of all those I serve and come in contact with. I want every person on planet earth to know this simple message and have the opportunity to experience optimal health through chiropractic. Here is a true to life experience of one of my patients who has benefited from chiropractic care and most recently benefited from care with the Pro-Adjuster. We hope our experiences empower you to reach your full health potential through chiropractic and the Pro-Adjuster.

As a Captain, of a treasure recovery vessel, my body has been dealt more than its fair share of hard knocks. For years I have had neck and back pain. Not just any pain but the kind that makes you feel you're about 80 years older than you really are. Over the years I have realized that this pain has depleted my life in many ways; it has left me agitated, somewhat depressed and has compromised my lifestyle. My medical doctors gave me some prescription drugs to use, and the pain was so severe that I used them. I felt I had to just get out of bed in the morning and physically make it down the docks to the boat. I became concerned about using the drugs, I was afraid I could become addicted to them. I knew I couldn't handle the constant pain so I was seeking an alternative. That is when I met Dr. Silva. He told me about chiropractic and I decided to give it a try. Following his recommendations for treatment, I was able to get to the point where the pain was non-existent. Then I had a set back. While riding on a lawn tractor, the mower blade caught the end of a palm frond and pulled the branch down, pinning me to the tractor. I was stuck there for a good ten minutes before I managed to get free. I thought for sure the pain was back and back to stay. Luckily at the same time as my accident, Dr. Silva was taking delivery of the Pro-Adjuster. After my very first adjustment with the Pro-Adjuster I could feel immediate relief and within two weeks I was fully recovered. Well let me just say this, I haven't felt this good in years. I am sleeping better, playing better and no longer suffer from the constant pain. I only wish I had tried this earlier. I think if more people would just try chiropractic they would be amazed with the results. The key is you need to give your spine proper attention and only chiropractic can give that. Thanks doc.

CAPTAIN DARRYL CUNNINGHAM

Crown Chiropractic Center
Dr. M. Travis Sizemore
Harrisonburg, Virginia

I grew up mostly in a home of nurses and my extended family had a lot of nurses. I played a lot of sports so there was a chance for a lot of injury and there was always the direction of wanting to be healthy so you could play.

We lived in a small town so I had never even really heard of a chiropractor. I didn't know what it was, what the word was even. Going to school I was in pre-dental, pre medicine. The whole time figuring I would be a dentist when I got out.

At some point I figured that I didn't want to look in peoples mouths all day for the rest of my life and I knew there had to be something out there different. Though I grew up in the home of a nurse, my philosophy was that I didn't want to take any medications, I didn't want any surgeries, I wanted to take the least amount of things possible, and try to do things as naturally as possible.

When I got to the point in college that I didn't want to be a dentist any more, I started looking around at other professions and other types of things to do with the health care field. I came upon the word Chiropractor. I really wasn't quite sure what to make of it because I had never heard of one before. As I mentioned earlier, playing sports mostly basketball, I was told I was really good and was really quick with my hands.

When I saw the definition of a Chiropractor as one who treats people and takes care of their health by the use of the hands without the use of drugs or surgery that just seemed to fit right in. I went to school on blind faith and immediately realized that was where I was supposed to be!

Here is a story from one of my patients:

Before I came to see Dr. Sizemore, I had been experiencing neck and back pain for over 30 years and more recently carpal tunnel and hip pain as well. I was told by one doctor that I have a crooked spine and that I also have osteoporosis.

I had tried a variety of methods to alleviate my pain. I had acupuncture, traditional chiropractic, took non-prescription medication, used ice and heat, tried bed rest, and even purchased a new mattress. All of those helped a little but I relied heavily upon using heat and traditional chiropractic treatments.

Sometimes the pain would get to the point that I would have a burning sensation and my extremities would "fall asleep". It was an unbearable discomfort.

My carpal tunnel and hip pain caused me to quit bowling and I slowed down a lot. I even had difficulty typing. I spent a lot of time resting. After trying so much, I believed someone my age would just have to learn to live with the pain. I became unhappy and frustrated with my life.

In July of 2002, Dr. Sizemore was having an open house for his clinic. I was new to the area and I was looking for a chiropractor to help me maintain my chiropractic schedule. This is when I was introduced to the Pro-Adjuster.

Like I said before, I had been to chiropractors in the past but no technique has ever worked the way the Pro-Adjuster has. I sleep better, I can do more around the house, and I just feel better. Not only can I bowl again but I even bought a new computer so I can type again.

The Pro-Adjuster is nearly painless but it works fast to make you feel better. I realized that someone my age can be helped and does not have to live with pain. I think everyone should use the Pro-Adjuster even if they have no major problems.

DIANE F. SIVACEK
RETIRED GOVERNMENT WORKER

Balanced Health Chiropractic Center, Inc.
Dr. Robert Smigelski
Rochester, MI

Before I became a chiropractor I was a naval aviator flying jets off of aircraft carriers for over seven years. After those years of service, I felt the need for a change in vocations. My wife and I were at a health fair and met a chiropractor. We started talking and he evaluated us. Being the typical male, I felt nothing was really wrong with me. Of course, I had some aches, pains and stiffness, especially in my neck and mid back region from all those landings on the carrier, but it was nothing I couldn't handle. After the evaluation and initial examination, I realized how much I needed care. After my chiropractor explained to me how important a properly functioning spine and nervous system was to my body, I knew I needed care.

As I received care in his office, I saw the passion and enthusiasm he had for his patients and for chiropractic. The benefits I received from chiropractic care and the love my chiropractor had for his vocation had a profound impact on me. I saw this as a way to help people heal and become healthy again — naturally. I decided then that I would become a chiropractor. I resigned from the Navy and started a new career path for me by going back to school at the age of 30. I will be forever grateful to my chiropractor for inspiring me to help others.

My purpose is to serve and help people through chiropractic care. By treating patients, writing articles and books, and giving lectures, my goal is to share my knowledge on health and natural healing with as many people as possible. I wish to educate all people on the total benefits of chiropractic health care. It is so much more than just simple relief from aches and pains. By having a fully functioning nervous system, a person can live their life to the fullest. Everyone can benefit from chiropractic care, from a one day old baby, to a 100 year old senior citizen, the life changing benefits are limitless.

One of my patients would like to share her chiropractic story with you. We hope our words help you understand how much you can be helped with chiropractic and the Pro-Adjuster.

I have been suffering with severe headaches since an automobile accident in February, 1984 in Colorado. After having thoracic surgery in Michigan in November of that year, I acquired paralysis of the right diaphragm and the right vocal cord. I was treated in Colorado by a neurologist, dentist and chiropractor for my neck and jaw region. When I returned to Michigan, I could not find a doctor or chiropractor to treat me for three months. Finally through a nurse friend, I was directed to a doctor who then referred me to a pulmonary specialist. I started to receive care for my pulmonary obstruction and speech therapy since my vocal cord was paralyzed. After that time I started chiropractic care on my own and have continued care ever since. When my chiropractor in Rochester closed her practice, I started seeing Dr. Rob.

Dr. Rob started mainly treating my headaches and with regular treatments, the headaches were beginning to become less frequent and not last as long. When Dr. Rob acquired the Pro-Adjuster, there was significant improvement in my condition. One day I started to get one of my worst headaches ever. It woke me up from my sleep at 4:45 a.m. and there was nothing I could do to relieve it. I took numerous medications including Fiorinal and even Imitrex and they had no effect on my headache. I got in to see Dr. Rob and after a treatment with the Pro-Adjuster I started to feel an immediate release of tension in my head and neck and the headache started to go away. I started to feel human again. If not for Dr. Rob and the Pro-Adjuster, I would have ended up in the emergency room because of the pain. My headaches have become less frequent and not as intense as they were previously. When I do suffer from a headache now, I know I will get the relief I need from Dr. Rob and the Pro-Adjuster. I know I will always have a problem with my neck and upper back area due to the car accident, shoulder replacement, and surgery, but with regular treatment on the Pro-Adjuster, I feel I will be able to get relief and live my life again.

ARLENE YEARN, TRAVEL AGENT

Smouse Chiropractic & Scoliosis Center
Gary F. Smouse, D.C., DACAN, CCSP
Sugar Land, Texas

After graduation from Texas Chiropractic College in 1975, I opened practice in a suburb of Houston. As one of the first chiropractors in the area, my practice grew rapidly and soon I was seeing a large volume of patients. I was quite pleased with the way my practice had grown in such a short period of time.

One day one of my mentors asked me my purpose in life. I started telling him my goals, at which time he stopped and said, "NO. What is your PURPOSE IN LIFE?"

I searched my soul for a long time looking for the answer. I even called my uncle who was responsible for introducing me to chiropractic since he himself was a chiropractor. His answer was very specific "to get sick people well with chiropractic care and to keep them well". For years I pondered this statement, with one question continuously coming up. "On what level"? This started to become apparent to me when my daughter showed signs of Idiopathic Rotatory Scoliosis at age eleven. Her spinal curves progressed rapidly, and I started to look for the answer to this disease. I was lead to a doctor who had the answers to my questions and a protocol to defeat this disease. I knew I was not taught this in college and I began to realize that my "purpose in life" was to educate as many doctors as possible about this program.

Things were going well in my teaching and in my private practice when suddenly I began having severe shoulder pain which made giving a manual adjustment too painful to perform. Now what? During Texas Chiropractic College Homecoming convention, I was working a booth for my Alumni Association when behold, across the aisle from me was my next answer — THE PRO-ADJUSTER.

For two days I watched every move, every adjustment that Dr. Maurice Pisciottano performed on doctors, their spouses, and chiropractic assistants. I talked with them after their adjustments and found they all had remarkable results. My research with the Pro-Adjuster and my scoliotic patients is ongoing, but at the time of this writing, the results are exceptional.

Lauren's story:

Lauren is a fifteen year old female who began seeking treatment from Dr. Smouse in March 2002. Lauren had been diagnosed with scoliosis at the age of twelve by her pediatrician. She was sent to an orthopedist and determined to not be of a severity required to treat at that time. Subsequent x-rays showed her still not severe enough for bracing; therefore, no treatment was indicated. We were not satisfied with this approach and wanted to do something to improve her spine curvature or, if nothing else, to at least give Lauren some relief from the low backache she often suffered.

The Internet provided information about scoliosis and led us to chiropractic doctors who were working to alleviate the problem of scoliosis. We began taking Lauren to a chiropractor who used standard adjustment methods and felt it was beneficial for bringing relief for her pain. However, her scoliosis seemed to be progressing and we were referred to Dr. Smouse to see if Lauren was a candidate for his treatment plan for scoliosis.

Treatment began in August 2002, with the Pro-Adjuster being an increasingly helpful tool in this recovery plan. Lauren's adjustments seem much easier on her physically, as she is small and thin for her age. The information on the screen is beneficial to me, as her parent, since I can see how the Pro-Adjuster has changed the alignment of her spine each time it is applied. This allows us to feel we are definitely moving in the right direction each time we watch her being adjusted.

At this point in time, we feel we have made the right choice in treatment plans for Lauren's condition and are very pleased with the progress she is making.

LAUREN DICKERSON'S MOM

Canonsburg Chiropractic Center
Dr. Jonathan F. Stein
Canonsburg, Pennsylvania

My involvement in chiropractic started while I was in college pursuing a degree in biology and pre-med, preparing to become a medical doctor. The summer of my second year was spent taking my mother to different doctors because of two rear end collisions that had occurred within one year. After countless attempts by many medical physicians, to treat her successfully, I made the observation that the only provider that was offering her any results was a chiropractor. I noticed with interest that this doctor had a completely different view of how the body works and how the nervous system function can promote healing as well as general good health. I thought that it was interesting to treat someone without medication, especially since it worked. However, I was going to become a maxillofacial surgeon, and continued on the path toward medicine.

The following year, I injured my back, and was treated (with great results) by a chiropractor. This offered me the chance to observe his practice, as well as the obvious enjoyment that came from his chosen profession. His job satisfaction, his quality of life, his relationships with his patients, etc. all influenced me as I pondered the direction to choose for my career. After discussion with him, and seeing the first-hand benefits that chiropractic offered, I went ahead and applied to Palmer College of Chiropractic and was accepted.

During my time at Palmer College, the late Dr. Walter Vernon Pierce, Sr. who was a pioneer in the systematic, scientific approach to treating the spine, instructed me. He did specific before and after analysis, which removed any doubt of the effectiveness and validity of the chiropractic adjustment. With the evolution of his research into what has become the Pro-Adjuster technology, I feel very certain about our ability to prove the concepts of chiropractic to put this health-based system into the mainstream of public knowledge instead of in the periphery. When the public understands what chiropractic is all about, vast numbers of people will be able to break free of encumbering reliance on overused medications, and therefore lead healthier and more productive lives.

My name is Patty Goodman, and I am a transportation attendant. I had been suffering with headaches and low back pain for many years, stemming back to some previous work in retail which entailed a good bit of moving boxes and merchandise. It got to the point that I was suffering with the severe headaches daily. I was trying heating pads for relief, as well as taking a large volume of Motrin. These methods of self-care really only gave short periods of relief, and the pain always returned. I began to "get used to the pain". I also began to have the realization that I was going to spend the rest of my life in pain. I felt as though I was twenty years older than I am, and the pain was beginning to interfere with my personal life. All of my family and friends would know when I was having a particularly bad day.

My husband had gone to a chiropractor in the past, and I decided to give it a try. I had nothing to lose after all…it was a last resort. I really never considered going to a chiropractor before this. Then, I made that big step, and then was evaluated by Dr. Stein. Shortly thereafter, the miracles began to occur. The first major breakthrough was to learn that my chronic low back pain was a result of a major misalignment in my neck! The next thing that happened was that my headaches disappeared. Really. From daily headaches to no headaches! I now have more energy than I have had in years. I now feel younger than I am! One last thing that I found very interesting was the fact that I used to have very cold hands and feet all the time. Even in the summertime I would have heavy socks on at home, and would complain about having cold hands. Well, it is the middle of winter and my hands and feet are warm! I am so glad I decided to become a chiropractic patient. The benefits have been outstanding!

PATTY GOODMAN

Strotheide Chiropractic
Dr. Jason Strotheide
Granite City, Illinois

Being the son of a chiropractor, I had always known the benefit of receiving chiropractic treatment. After all, I noticed that I was hardly ever sick when all of my friends were and I noticed that my family didn't take nearly as much medicine as all of the other families. However, it wasn't until I was 15 years old that I truly learned just how chiropractic can change a person's life. You see, I was a competitive hockey player. In a split second, my life changed. I was checked from behind, driving my head into the boards. I hit so hard, I was unconscious for a few seconds. Upon getting up, I knew I had been hurt. Within 20 seconds, I experienced my first ever headache. Unfortunately, this headache did not go away. In fact it worsened! My headaches got so bad that I actually developed insomnia due to the pain and I went from a nearly straight "A" student to having to struggle just to get 'B's' and 'C's'. When I say my life was changing, I mean it was changing, and not for the better. One day a miracle occurred. My father gave me a chiropractic adjustment to my upper neck and within 20 minutes my headache was gone. It was at that point that I knew I wanted to help people get better and to share with them my "chiropractic story".

Because of this, my purpose is to help as many people as possible experience the benefits of chiropractic care and to educate my patients about what I do. I strive to help people realize that their body does not always need pills and potions and to recognize the fact that we all have the ability of our body to heal itself, as long as we have a properly functioning nervous system. After all, the power that made the body heals the body. It is as simple as that!

It all began in June of 2001. Having suffered with severe back pain for over 20 years and severe respiratory problems, including chronic bronchitis and severe asthma, my entire life, my health and life began to change. You see, June of 2001 was my first visit to Dr. Strotheide's office and my first experience with the Pro-Adjuster.

During my life, I have been given all types of treatment for my asthma. I've received shots, breathing treatments, steroids and inhalers. I have been hospitalized numerous times due to the inability to control my respiratory problems. For my back, I've been put on bed rest for weeks, taken all kinds of pain medications and muscle relaxers, received steroid injection to my spine, been to physical therapy, been to pain management, and in 1984, I actually had back surgery. The shame of it is that none of it worked.

I have had all of these treatments, spent all of that time and money, and missed so much of life due to my health problems, and nothing worked. I felt like I was going to have to live like this for the rest of my life. I wound up frustrated and eventually suffered clinical depression due to the pain I was in.

One day, I was talking to a friend of mine who suggested that I go to see a chiropractor. I told her there was no way I was going to have somebody twist my neck and pop my back. I told her I was afraid they would hurt me due to the back surgery. My friend assured me this would not happen. She told me that Dr. Strotheide uses a machine called the Pro-Adjuster and that he was able to tell what was wrong and treat the problem area without twisting, popping, and most importantly, safely without pain.

I have to say she was right. Dr. Strotheide and the Pro-Adjuster changed my life. I can now walk up and down stairs, shop and stand without pain. My breathing is also better. I remember the first time Dr. Strotheide did the "Breathing Protocol". I was in the middle of an asthma attack and had been suffering with bronchitis for about 2 weeks. When he came into the room, he noticed I was not breathing right. He evaluated my spine, worked on my back, told me to sit up and take a deep breath. When I did, I was able to take a full breath without wheezing and without coughing.

There are not enough good things I can say about Dr. Strotheide and the Pro-Adjuster. Take it from a skeptic, it's the best thing you will ever do for yourself!

INA JOHNSON

Wright Chiropractic
Dr. Jerrod Wright
Southlake, Texas

When I was in high school, I began getting headaches occasionally. The headaches became more frequent and intense after I graduated. By my second year in college, I was having two to three headaches a week. They were interfering with my studying and with my extra curricular activities. They were messing with my life. I sought medical help, but became frustrated when all they did was give me medication (which didn't help). No one seemed to be interested in why these headaches began in the first place; they just wanted to mask the pain with drugs. Something had to change. A friend suggested chiropractic. The chiropractor took a history and found that I had been knocked unconscious twice (football/jet ski) and was in a pretty bad car wreck a few years before the headaches began. He told me there was a good chance I had some malfunctions in my spine, called subluxations that were causing my headaches. He did an examination, found two places in the top of my neck that were fixated, and took some x-rays. He then began correcting the subluxated areas. He wasn't even interested in the headaches anymore. He found the cause and knew if he corrected the cause, the symptoms (headaches) would go away. They did! That chiropractor gave my life back to me. That's priceless! I am a chiropractor myself now. I thank God that I have the best job in the world. I get to watch miraculous things happen in people's lives every single day and know that I had a part in it. The greatest reward is seeing hope in the eyes of people who previously had no hope. That is why I do what I do. To give hope to the hopeless by removing nerve interference in the body and letting the body do its job; heal itself! It really is as simple as that. Our bodies were designed to heal themselves, given that there is no interference. Most of my patients have come to me as a last resort and that's a shame. They have usually spent a lot of time and lot of money trying to get well the so called "traditional" way and have a tough time believing in something else. That's why I use the Pro-Adjuster. It shows people exactly where their problem is. Seeing is believing. The treatment results are also much quicker, and are completely painless. After a few treatments I usually hear, "I wish I would have done this a long time ago". I wish they would have too. That's the reason for this book.

I had been suffering from multiple alignment/repair problems, including shoulders, neck, lower back and knee issues. I had been in several car accidents with whiplash damage, and I also had fibromyalgia as a result of an autoimmune disease. Over the years, I have tried virtually all modalities besides traditional medicine and chiropractic — including massage, physical therapy, ice, heat, acupuncture, reflexology, allergy antigens, deep tissue work, herbal body wraps, magnets, herbal products, the chi machine and other equipment aimed at deep tissue repair, Rolfing, aromatherapy and yoga. Of the above, I experienced some relief from everything except traditional medicine and the magnets, but nothing gave me the complete pain relief. I had the greatest benefit from chiropractic with deep tissue massage, Rolfing and yoga. I have found that a positive mental attitude combined with a core of supportive structural work and yoga now results in complete pain management. At one time I was sure there was NO relief for me, as I had spent tens of thousands of dollars and years in search of relief. My chronic pain prevented proper sleep and even concentration. There are lots of things I bypassed doing because of my condition. In my 20's and 30's I had trouble walking up a flight of stairs. I felt like I was in my 70's. I have sought chiropractic care on a regular basis all my life as a way to allow me to tolerate the pain. When Dr. Wright got the Pro-Adjuster, I was very pleased after my first treatment, because the adjustment seemed more evenly balanced and also capable of affecting my delicate skeletal structure in a more gentle way while still accomplishing the skeletal movement I needed. I have improved my flexibility, and can now do the yoga headstand on my elbows. I also have a huge improvement in range of motion in my neck. One of the best benefits for me is that I am now not tense about the adjustment process from fear of the procedure itself (my chronic pain always made adjustments very uncomfortable before). I also feel that the Pro-Adjuster makes the chiropractic process much more scientific and trackable. I can truly say that Dr. Wright and the Pro-Adjuster have made all the difference in my quality of life.

EILEEN SILVA,
METABOLIC WEIGHT CONTROL AND
BODY BALANCING SPECIALIST

Canonsburg Chiropractic Center
Dr. Laurel Gretz-Pisciottano
Canonsburg, Pennsylvannia

Back in 1946, I was involved in an automobile accident. At the time I thought I was not injured, and therefore received no follow-up care and did not go to the hospital to be evaluated. In 1964, I began to have dizzy spells. I had such balance difficulties that I could not walk for a few steps without help. I went to the medical doctor several times. He would send me to the hospital, I would be admitted, then have tests, and I would be released with "nerve pills" to take. There was never any answer or reason that this would happen to me. The dizziness would go away for a time, but it would always come back. I would become so bad that I would have to crawl around the house. I missed a good bit of work, and eventually, I did have to quit my position in 1978. In 1983, a relative told me that they had seen a chiropractor, and had good results. I was skeptical as I had had so many medical examinations and tests, and there was never a solution to the problem. The chiropractor did find a problem however, and began treating me several times per week for two months. I was actually able to return to work after that series of treatment, and it was done with no drugs. I had virtually no dizziness or balance problems except occasionally when lying down. I did continue to have maintenance care for many years, however, at times I would have difficulty laying down for the treatment, and would become sore from the adjustments. Then a wonderful thing happened. The clinic began to utilize a new technology called the Pro-Adjuster. This allowed me to sit through the entire treatment, and did not involve any twisting of my neck whatsoever. I never doubted the benefits of chiropractic care, however this was a new added bonus…I didn't have to 'get through' the treatments anymore. It was comfortable, easy, and I no longer had to lay flat. I have a totally new outlook on life now. I am now able to do many of the things that I missed out on for so many years. I don't have to take medication, and I feel better than I have in years. I tell everyone I know about the Pro-Adjuster. Anyone that is having pains anywhere in his or her body should see a chiropractor. The public should keep in mind that like me, chiropractic problems don't have to involve pain.

BETTY FRYE

Barrett Chiropractic Clinic, P.C.
Dr. Richard F. Barrett
Missouri City, Texas

My problems started in 1984 with a work injury. I caught a file box that was falling from the top of a shelf while I was kneeling below getting something out of another drawer. Instincts made me reach up to protect my head. The box weighed about 40 pounds and moved my shoulder out of its joint.

I went to a chiropractor first who referred me to a doctor specializing in this injury. Surgery was required; in fact I had three surgeries during the next three years. While recuperating from my last surgery we were rear ended at a red light. I ended up with severe whiplash then I began to get migraines and vision problems that were quite severe. The doctor at Kaiser Permanente thought it might be an after effect due to the whiplash.

Since I could not take aspirin or any anti-inflammatory medicine due to achalasia, which effects my esophagus, there was not much he could do. After five weeks of headaches I decided to go back to a chiropractor to find some relief. The chiropractor was able to help me. The migraines went away, I had less pain, but my mobility did not improve. I could only turn my head slightly to either side leaning the head to the right or left was impossible. I only had eleven- percent mobility in my neck. Before the work injury I was always into sports and lots of outdoor activities. The injuries prevented me from doing any activities I was used to. Then my company transferred me to Texas and I was without a chiropractor.

In October I was having severe back and neck pain including pain in all joints due to activities.

In October we had a health fair at work. A referral service for chiropractic was present. I had been looking for a chiropractor because I always had gotten pain relief. I was having severe back and neck pain including pain in all joints due to arthritis. The lady recommended Dr. Barrett, she told me he was using a device that was new and has very good results.

I was reluctant to go to just any chiropractor so I felt better with a referral. I expected to get the usual pain relief; however no improvement in mobility. After so many years I just did not think it could improve. I was so impressed when I saw the Pro-Adjuster equipment. It looked like an improvement over some of the manual tools used.

Now three months later, no back pains. However, the best is, I can move my neck and now look over my shoulder instead of turning my whole body! It makes driving a car much safer. If you ever tried backing up without turning your neck you know what I mean. I used to have to unbuckle the seat belt in order to turn to see backing out of a parking space.

I still will be dealing with some pain due to arthritis and my mobility may never be 100 percent, but I would not bet on this assumption because of the improvement just after three months. I may even try playing golf again, before I could not turn my neck to see the ball. Now who knows — the sky is the limit.

I now know not to give up. If something does not work, something else might. The Pro-Adjuster seems to work even in cases where manual manipulations were not able to attain any improvement. Before I went to chiropractic not to get worse, now I am going to get better.

If you have similar problems try the Pro-Adjuster treatment. You will be surprised with the results! Thank you Dr. Barrett!

URSULA HAYES, CONSULTANT

I first came to Pisciottano Chiropractic Clinic when my neck was so painful that I could hardly turn it from side to side. The movement of turning my head was limited. At times, something in my neck would "lock" completely and I couldn't move my head at all! The pain was so severe that I would scream if someone touched my back. These symptoms had plagued me for years. I was treated by another Chiropractor for this condition, however he did not explain to me what he was going to be doing, nor did I have a complete treatment plan. With this Chiropractor I had some relief of pain but little increase in neck movement. All of my symptoms returned and there was no follow-up care offered.

Within three weeks of treatment with the Pro-Adjuster, the motion in my neck has returned and my neck has not "locked" at all. The pain in my knee has totally disappeared. This office is very professional and the doctors and staff are very thorough in explaining everything and setting up a treatment plan.

- NANCY LEVKUS

Chapter Eleven

Chiropractic Outreach – Pro-Adjusting the World

The Pro-Adjuster is a valuable precision instrument that allows the chiropractor to effectively treat spinal health related problems. The instrument is being used world wide in countries like Spain, Australia, and Japan to name a few. It also has been effectively used in the field on medical missionary work. The portability of the equipment means that doctors can perform outreach into world communities and still deliver the same high level of analysis and treatment that they would in their own offices. Dr. Barrett found many cases on his routine medical mission trip to Mexico that were best served with the Pro-Adjuster rather than standard manual manipulations. Patients with juvenile rheumatoid arthritis, severe osteoporosis, severe degenerative joint disease and wheel chair bound individuals were among these.

Spreading the chiropractic natural healing message globally is a high priority. Every person young or old, rich or poor, regardless of ideology, religious orientation or political persuasion has a right to basic human equality and ultimately equal access to the best healthcare. It is deplorable that there are multitudes of people in the world who are denied basic care because they are so poor. The Pro-Adjuster is an exceptional tool to deliver a higher standard of care to these people. The patients are remarkably accepting of the new technology. They put their full trust in the doctors and are extremely grateful of the care they receive. The following photographs demonstrate Dr. Barrett treating patients with the Pro-Adjuster in a remote tropical area of Mexico.

29 year old patient
with juvenile
rheumatoid arthritis

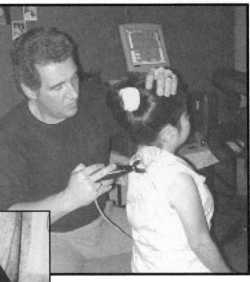

Treating wheelchair
bound patient

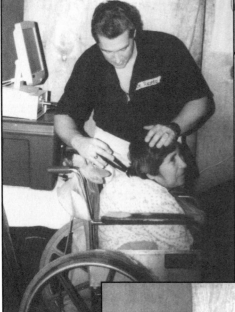

Fragile patient
over 100 years old!
Suffers from osteoporosis
and severe degenerative
joint disease

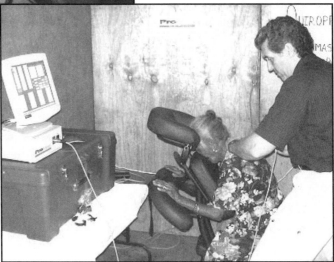

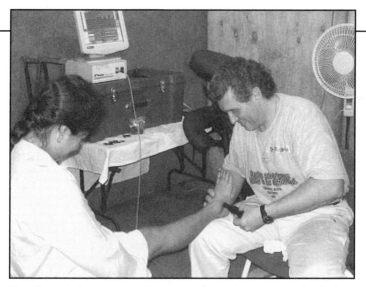

The Pro-Adjuster works great for other musculoskeletal problems including extremities.

Treating patients on a mission can be very difficult. The conditions and circumstances are less than ideal. In fact, they are quite extreme. Not only for the doctors but especially for the people. It is not uncommon for families to walk hours to days to receive care. When they arrive, some before daylight, they then have to wait hours more for treatment. Most have little food and drink or the money to buy it. With temperatures reaching the high 90's it can be quite uncomfortable. Especially if one is in pain, and hundreds of people are waiting. Without the luxury of diagnostic equipment such as an X-ray unit, the doctors have to rely highly on their diagnostic skills and be careful with their treatments. However, using the Pro-Adjuster is a tremendous asset. It performs a spinal analysis which is diagnostic and delivers an exact treatment. This not only gives the patient a high level of confidence but increases the certainty of the doctor. With safety, accuracy and precision a perfect adjustment can be delivered each and every time. Regardless of the age or condition of the patient. Though the conditions are harsh with high temperatures and power fluctuations, the Pro-Adjuster worked flawlessly. Within a clinical setting you can always be assured of a perfect treatment. The environment will be friendly, the staff caring, and the surroundings comfortable and ideal. The doctors of chiropractic are highly skilled and understand not only the function of your body but the proper way to treat your spine. As the analysis and treatment of your spine takes place you can be assured that you will be comfortable in the Pro-Adjuster chair. Children, adults, athletes, those with fragile spines, postsurgical patients, injured people and the elderly all enjoy and benefit from their Pro-Adjuster chiropractic treatments.

The following photographs show how the patients are at ease as Dr. Pisciottano delivers a Pro-Adjuster chiropractic treatment.

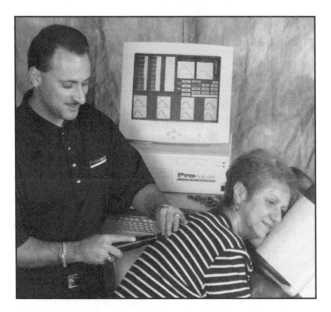

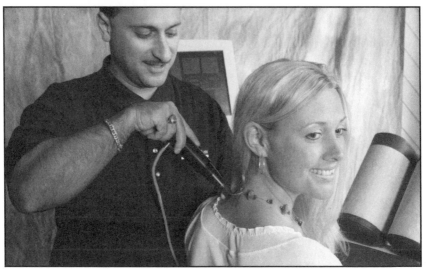

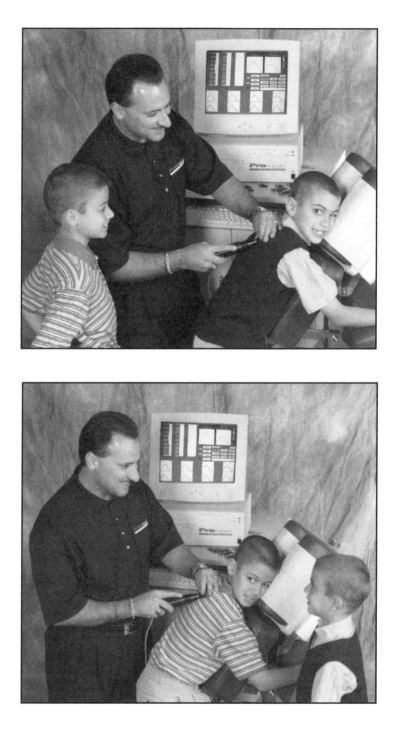

This book was designed to expand your thinking and view health, healing and vitality in a whole new way. It is critical that you act on this newfound knowledge, so that you may begin to experience a new level of health and achieve the Peak Performance that your body was designed for. Much can be accomplished with the right guidance at home and that is why you were given the tools in several chapters to begin the work at home. Any precision instrument, whether it is a watch, a race car or a human body, needs to be evaluated and fine tuned by experts.

As you are aware, your nervous system is the vital and critical component to the correct functioning of your entire body. Hopefully you now understand how the proper use of chiropractic care can and will relieve your pain and help you achieve a never before realized level of health. As a doctor of chiropractic we want you to know miracles can happen. Millions of people throughout the world are benefiting from chiropractic care.

Now with the great advance in technology, chiropractic through the use of the Pro-Adjuster will safely, painlessly reach millions more. If you have yet to experience what others already know, we urge you to try chiropractic, the Pro-Adjuster way, right now. It is not a mistake that this book is in your hands. There is purpose and reason behind all things.

If you are currently a patient and are experiencing the benefit of chiropractic care, then pass this book on to someone who may be complaining of a health concern. If you are not currently receiving chiropractic care, then please use this as an opportunity to see if you can be helped.

You have now come to the end of the journey and we would like to suggest some steps to take next. You may be in one of the following categories:

1) A new or existing patient seeing a chiropractor with the Pro-Adjuster

2) Previous chiropractic patient

3) Never sought chiropractic care before

4) Current chiropractic patient receiving manual or other forms of treatment

Our wish is that you, your family, and friends attain health and achieve pain relief the safest and most advanced way possible. We hope that you have had all your questions answered and understand the benefits of chiropractic and the Pro-Adjuster. We look forward to any comments you might have.

If you are in:

Category 1-We request that you share the knowledge you have gained with another person. Please attain a book for them either from your Pro-Adjuster doctor's office or directly from Pro-Solutions at 1-877- 942-4284.

Category 2-If you have not had chiropractic care in over six months we strongly advise you to get to a chiropractor and have your nervous system reevaluated and treated. Regular maintenance adjustments of your nervous system will help you maintain health. If you no longer have a chiropractor, find a Pro-Adjuster doctor and experience a new type of evaluation, analysis and treatment. We also encourage you to share your new knowledge and help another person to enhance their life. Please attain another book from a Pro-Adjuster doctor or directly from Pro- Solutions at 1-877-942-4284. You can also reach us on the web at www.Pro-Adjuster.com.

Category 3- You are urged to experience what all of us already know. Healing naturally is the best way to treat yourself. Call us at Pro-Solutions directly 1-877- 942-4284 or contact us through e-mail if you need help finding a Pro-Adjuster doctor. The knowledge you have gained needs to be shared to help another in need. Please attain another copy of this book and give it to someone who you believe could benefit from it.

Category 4-You now are aware of a different kind of treatment but please continue with the care you are currently receiving. You will benefit greatly. Please share this book with your doctor. He or she may very well be interested in testing the Pro-Adjuster in their office. They can reach us at Pro-Solutions 1-877- 942-4284. We also ask that you continue to spread the chiropractic message with others who you believe have an unwanted health condition. Please attain another book for them. You can get a copy directly from Pro Solutions at 1-877-942-4284.

Thank you for allowing all of us to come into your life, and giving us one of your most precious assets-your time! We wish you great health naturally!

Maurice Pisciottano, D.C.   Richard F. Barrett, D.C.

Laurel Gretz-Pisciottano, D.C.   Jason L. Strotheide, D.C.

Geno A. Pisciottano, D.C.   Joseph Porreca, D.C.

Masa Yamasaki, D.C.   Gary Smouse, D.C.

Steve Arculeo,D.C.   Shaun R. Gifford, D.C.

Matt Goldman, D.C.   Jill Howe, D.C.

Rebecca Kloczkowski, D.C.   Kevin Laster, D.C.

James Maggio, D.C.   Sam Nia, D.C.

Michele E. Quam, D.C.   Peter G. Phillips, D.C.

John L. Silva, D.C.   Donald F. Riefer, D.C.

Rob Smigelski, D.C.   Travis Sizemore, D.C.

Jerrod Wright, D.C.   Jonathan F. Stein, D.C.

Contributing Writers

Dr. Steve Arculeo is the director of Peak Performance Health Care Center in Old Town, Chicago. The innovative combination of Computerized Chiropractic Care with the Pro-Adjuster, Patient-Active Physical Therapy and Conservative Medical Care, has made his center well known for its success in the natural care of headaches, back pain and athletic injuries. As the first chiropractic physician to speak at the American Medical Association headquarters, he is actively involved in the research and advancement of natural health care. He has cared for professional baseball and football players as well as world-class marathoners and tri-athletes. He has worked with Ballet Chicago and as the team physician for the Jesse White Tumbling Team, and is on the executive board of directors of *We Are Concerned,* a Chicago nonprofit health improvement organization. Dr. Arculeo is also a health consultant for NBC News, WGN News, and *Crain's Chicago Business* magazine. He has authored clinical research papers on headaches and back pain and two health columns for local newspapers.

Peak Performance Health Care Center
1749 N. Wells Street, Chicago, IL 60614
Phone (312) 440-9646

Dr. Shaun R. Gifford is a graduate of Northwestern College of Chiropractic in Bloomington, MN. He completed his undergraduate studies at Brigham Young University in Idaho. He received his Bachelor of Science degree in Human Services from Northwestern College of Chiropractic. He currently resides in Bloomington with his wife Veronica and young daughter Katherine. He volunteers as a Boy Scout Master for Troop 192. He enjoys being outdoors camping, hiking or fishing. Current hobbies include fencing and archery.

Ruhland Chiropractic Clinic
5402 W. Old Shakopee Road, Bloomington, Minnesota 55437
Phone (952) 884-1507

Dr. Matt Goldman earned his Bachelors Degree from the University of Colorado. He received his Masters in Chiropractic Sports Sciences and his Doctor of Chiropractic degrees from Life University where he also worked with the soccer and rugby teams for the Department of Sports Chiropractic as the team chiropractor. Dr. Goldman is board certified from the International Academy of Neuromuscular Therapy and is a member of the International Federation of Sports Chiropractic. Dr. Goldman's philosophy of treating patients combines the detection with the correction of biomechanical and neurological stressors in the body. Pro-Solutions Advisory Board Member

Progressive Healthcare
4000 Waterdam Plaza, Suite 240
McMurray, Pennsylvania 15317
Phone (724) 942-4444

Dr. Laurel Gretz-Pisciottano attended the Indiana University of Pennsylvania and Palmer College of Chiropractic. Dr. Gretz obtained her Bachelor of Science degree in Human Biology and her Doctorate of Chiropractic degree in 1989. She conducted various research projects during her clinical experience at Palmer College, and continues to be involved in the research and development of technique and documentation, and is certified in Pro-Adjuster technique. Dr. Gretz is a second generation chiropractor and is currently in private practice in Canonsburg, Pennsylvania. Pro-Solutions Advisory Board Member

Canonsburg Chiropractic Center
326 West Pike Street
Canonsburg, Pennsylvania 15317
Phone (724) 745-3525

Dr. Jill Howe attended Iowa State University for her undergraduate studies. She is a 1991 graduate of the National College of Chiropractic where she received the degree of Doctor of Chiropractic. She has been in practice for eleven years and currently practices in Crystal Lake, Illinois (a suburb 11/2 hours northwest of Chicago).

Dynamic Family Health Center
7105 Virginia Road #24
Crystal Lake, Illinois 60014
Phone (815) 477-8844

Dr. Rebecca Ulsh Kloczkowski graduated summa cum laude from Palmer College in 1984. She received numerous scholarships and awards during her years at Palmer. Establishing the Montgomery Chiropractic and Wellness Center in 1986, she rapidly developed her practice by treating all age groups from infants to the elderly. She holds numerous certifications including a variety of specialized treatments as the result of over 1,000 hours of additional training. She is a member of 12 professional associations and holds licenses in the states of Ohio and California. Her community work has included the U.C. Medical Student Program and participation in many fundraisers to benefit organizations such as the American Cancer Society, American Heart Association, and Alzheimer's Association. Dr. Rebecca and her husband are active members of their church and apply their faith to all aspects of their lives. She believes health is gift that requires a faithful attitude, proper diet and rest, and regular chiropractic care.

Montgomery Chiropractic
9200 Montgomery Road, Suite 10B
Cincinnati, Ohio 45242
Phone (513) 791-1888

Dr. Kevin Laster received his Doctorate of Chiropractic from Sherman College of Chiropractic in South Carolina in June of 1989. While attending college he held the position of vice-president of the student International Chiropractic Association. Additionally he performed duties as the class representative for the Honor Council. Since receiving his degree, Dr. Laster has been very involved in his community. He assists his church with both food and clothing drives. Dr. Laster counsels his patients on dietary and nutritional components of their health programs that eliminate the need for many drugs. He enjoys treating children and is a continual advocate for chiropractic and natural healing in his community.

Progressive Healthcare
4000 Waterdam Plaza, Suite 240
McMurray, Pennsylvania 15317
Phone (724) 942-4444

Dr. James Maggio is a chiropractor residing in Virginia Beach. Dr. Maggio is originally from Long Island, New York. He attended St. Joseph's College where he received his Bachelor of Science. After completing a degree in Biology he attended Cleveland Chiropractic College in Kansas City where he received his degree in chiropractic. Dr. Maggio's practice is located on Witchduck Road and he currently is providing community services to the public by having Self Help Workshops. Dr. Maggio has provided health programs for the Virginia Beach school system, police departments and fire departments. His practice specializes in health and wellness and is one of only 200 doctors in the world that utilizes the fully computerized Pro-Adjusting chiropractic system.

Chiropractic Center of Virginia Beach
114 South Witchduck Road
Virginia Beach, Virginia 23461
Phone (757) 473-9900

Dr. Sam Nia completed his undergraduate studies at East Tennessee State University. He then earned his Doctorate of Chiropractic degree from Life Chiropractic University. He specializes in upper cervical specific care. Dr. Nia continues to pursue his purpose in life by improving the health and well being of people around the world whether involved in mission trips or presenting over 1000 educational lectures for major corporations and private groups. He is a proud and recipient of the "Foreign Messenger Award" for chiropractic mission trip services.

Back To Action Chiropractic
6030 Bethelview Road, Unit 502
Cumming, Georgia 30040
Phone (770) 888-8292

Dr. Peter G. Phillips practices in Vancouver, Washington. He received his Doctor of Chiropractic degree from Palmer College of Chiropractic in 1987. Dr. Phillips is very active in Chiropractic, both in his local community and throughout Washington State. He has served as President of the local Chiropractic society and has twice been selected as Chiropractor of the year. Dr. Phillips is very active in his community and his church. "Chiropractic allows me to help sick people get well naturally without the use of drugs or surgery". Dr. Phillips strives to have the best equipment available in chiropractic and attends many seminars throughout the country to receive first hand knowledge of the modern advancements in chiropractic.

Dr. Peter G. Phillips, Chiropractor
8312 E. Mill Plain Boulevard
Vancouver, WA 98664
Phone (360) 694-1118

Dr. Geno A. Pisciottano, Director of Progressive Health Care Clinics, is a noted technique instructor and has been instrumental in the development of an advanced chiropractic adjusting chair. Since graduating from Palmer College of Chiropractic, he has been a driving force in the demanding Medical Necessity Documentation arena. Because of his knowledge, Dr. Pisciottano is considered an expert in this field. He consults with hundreds of doctors and writes the documentation software language for key documentation programs on the market. Dr. Pisciottano has developed several patient management systems that can be duplicated to benefit any practice. Along with his brother, Dr. Maurice A. Pisciottano, Dr. Geno Pisciottano has helped pioneer the success of computerized technology in the field of chiropractic. Pro-Solutions Advisory Board Member

Progressive Healthcare
4000 Waterdam Plaza, Suite 240
McMurray, Pennsylvania 15317
Phone (724) 942-4444

Dr. Joseph Porreca completed his undergraduate work, in which he received his Bachelor of Science Degree in Biology, at California University of Pennsylvania. He then went on to earn his Doctor of Chiropractic Degree from Palmer College of Chiropractic in Davenport, Iowa. Dr. Porreca graduated from Palmer College Summa cum Laude and was inducted into the academic honor society Pi Tau Delta. Dr. Porreca makes himself available on a regular basis to give lectures for the general public in order to improve the health of those in his community.

Porreca Chiropractic Center, Inc.
1100 Fayette Avenue
Belle Vernon, Pennsylvania 15012
Phone (724) 929-6077

Dr. Michele Elise Quam received her Doctorate Degree from Los Angeles College of Chiropractic where she graduated with honors in 1992. She has been practicing in Fullerton, CA since 1994. Since graduating, she has written numerous articles concerning health and wellness. Dr. Quam lectures on health related topics at local clubs and businesses. Chiropractic is a second career for her. So unlike the phone company job that she fell into, chiropractic is the career that she finally had the opportunity to choose. Now Dr. Quam does what she has a strong passion and desire to do, which is to help others reach optimal health through natural chiropractic care.

Fullerton Chiropractic Wellness Center
137 W. Chapman Avenue
Fullerton, CA 92832
Phone (714) 525-5225

Dr. Donald F. Riefer practices in Cedartown, Georgia. He has a Bachelor of Science Degree in nutrition and is currently working on his Masters in nutrition. He graduated from Life University Chiropractic College in 1997. Dr. Riefer has treated thousands of patients successfully including several professional athletes. He promotes community health and well being and patient education through weekly lectures on chiropractic and nutrition. He is also on the Board of Regents for the Carpal Tunnel Relief Foundation. Dr. Riefer's philosophy on chiropractic is that healing comes from **above down inside out** which is why he named his practice **ADIO** Chiropractic Center.

ADIO Chiropractic Center
321 West Avenue, Suite A
Cedartown, Georgia 30125
Phone (770) 749-8701

Dr. John L. Silva is an honors graduate from Barry University in Miami, where he received his pre-medical degree. Dr. Silva also graduated with honors from Life University, the world's largest Chiropractic College. While attending Life University, he served as an officer with the Student Alumni Association and traveled the country extensively attending chiropractic technique seminars. Dr. Silva continues to advance his knowledge of chiropractic in a wellness model by attending post-graduate seminars nationwide. He is a member of the International Chiropractic Association and the Chiropractic Leadership Alliance. One of his most memorable chiropractic experiences was serving as an honorary doctor on a mission trip to Pachuca, Mexico in July 2000. Through his studies and passion for discovering all things healthy, he is able to provide his patients with the most advanced and sophisticated diagnostic and treatment instruments available in Chiropractic today.

Silva Family Chiropractic
6668 South U.S. Hwy 1
Port St. Lucie, FL 34952
Phone (772) 215-0153

Dr. M. Travis Sizemore attended Marshall University in Huntington, West Virginia where he obtained his Bachelor of Science degree in biology. He then went on to Logan College of Chiropractic in Chesterfield, Missouri where he obtained another Bachelor of Science degree in human biology and then his Doctor of Chiropractic. Dr. Sizemore currently owns an office in Harrisonburg, Virginia that has been open for close to a year now. This office has been using the Pro-Adjuster since opening day!

Crown Chiropractic Center
4032 Quarles Court
Harrisonburg, Virginia 22801
Phone (540) 432-5577

Dr. Robert Smigelski attended the University of Florida and received his Bachelor of Science in Mathematics in 1986. After graduation, he was commissioned in the U.S. Navy and became a Naval Flight Officer. After serving 7 years in the Navy, Dr. Smigelski attended Palmer College of Chiropractic in Davenport, IA. He graduated in 1998 with high honors, finishing 3rd out of a class of 200. While attending Palmer College, he was a Presidential Scholar, and selected to the Vogt Leadership Society, the All American Scholar Society, Who's Who Among American Colleges and Universities and was President of Pi Tau Delta, the Chiropractic Honor Fraternity. Presently, he is president of Balanced Health Chiropractic Center, Inc. with offices in Rochester and Farmington Hills, MI. He is happily married to Teresa, his wife of 14 years, and they have two wonderful children, Michael Edmund, age 4 and Grace Evelyn, age 4 months.

Balanced Health Chiropractic Center, Inc.
134 W. University Suite 126
Rochester, Michigan 48307
Phone (248) 656-5900

Dr. Gary F. Smouse is a 1975 graduate of Texas Chiropractic College. He is certified in Chiropractic Sports Practitioner and a Diplomate American Chiropractic Academy of Neurology. For over a decade, Dr. Smouse has focused on implementing a comprehensive protocol for treating scoliosis. He is a nationally recognized author, teacher and presenter. Dr. Smouse has received numerous awards for his tireless efforts with his alumni, state and local chiropractic associations. Dr. Smouse is married with two children, one of which is about to graduate from Texas Chiropractic College. He maintains a busy practice in Sugar Land, Texas. Pro-Solutions Advisory Board Member

Smouse Chiropractic and Scoliosis Center
14015 S. W. Freeway, Suite 9
Sugar Land, Texas 77478
Phone (281) 494-5144

Dr. Jonathan F. Stein obtained his Bachelor of Science Degree (magna cum laude) from Indiana University of Pennsylvania in Biology and Pre-Med. He went on to graduate with a Doctorate of Chiropractic from the Palmer College of Chiropractic, summa cum laude in 1988. Dr. Stein is certified in Video fluoroscopy and the Pro-Adjuster technique, and is currently on staff with Pro-Solutions for Chiropractic as an instructor. Pro-Solutions Advisory Board Member

Canonsburg Chiropractic Center
326 West Pike Street
Canonsburg, Pennsylvania 15317
Phone (724) 745-3525

Dr. Jason L. Strotheide is a second generation chiropractor who maintains a high volume practice in Granite City, Illinois. Since graduating from Logan College of Chiropractic in 1993, Dr. Strotheide has worked on blending his chiropractic philosophy, knowledge of clinical biomechanics, anatomy and the technological advancements in chiropractic to better educate his patients and improve his retention. He has also been instrumental in documenting the need for continued care to insurance companies, peer reviewers, and in litigation scenarios. Dr. Strotheide is a noted lecturer on the topics of Health Care Compliance, Documentation, and Medical Necessity. He has spoken to hundreds of doctors regarding these topics. Dr. Strotheide has been instrumental in making the Pro-Adjuster technology a part of the continuing education curriculum at the Logan College of Chiropractic. Dr. Strotheide has been a Pro-Solutions Continuing Education Faculty member for the past two years. Pro-Solutions Advisory Board Member

Strotheide Chiropractic
3412 Nameoki Road
Granite City, Illinois 62040
Phone (618) 876-7800

Dr. Jerrod Wright graduated from Parker College of Chiropractic in January 1996 in the top ten percent of his class with a Doctorate Degree in Chiropractic and a Bachelor of Science Degree in Anatomy. His passion was to become a "family doctor" of wellness. He opened his doors three months after graduating in Southlake, Texas and became just that. Today, Dr. Wright treats hundreds of families from newborn children to grandparents. He utilizes nutrition, exercise and chiropractic care to keep his patients healthy and their bodies functioning at the highest level.

Wright Chiropractic
502 North Carroll
Southlake, TX 76092
Phone (817) 488-4186

Dr. Masa Yamasaki is a 1971 graduate from the Meize Oriental School of Medicine in Japan. In 1976, he graduated from Mitzu Shiwokowa Chiropractic School. He is authorized to practice both medicine and chiropractic in Japan. Dr. Masa is one of the most highly respected doctors in the world in the use of instrument adjusting. He travels across the world to work with Dr. Maurice Pisciottano to help develop new techniques for the Pro-Adjuster System. Dr. Masa started the Susaki City Clinic in 1974, and then opened the Kochi Chiropractic Clinic in 1988. Pro-Solutions Advisory Board Member

Phone 011-(888) 883-2544

Order the following inspirational, educational books and products:

Improve Your Health Pro-Actively
by Dr. Maurice A. Pisciottano & Dr. Richard F. Barrett . . . $12.95
    Also available on audio cassette $12.95

Personal Financial Freedom (CD and Booklet)
by Dr. Maurice A. Pisciottano $69.95

Pro-Peak Performance, Productivity and Energy Enhancements (CD)
by Dr. Maurice A. Pisciottano $69.95

Dare to Break Through the Pain; A Guide to Eliminating Back & Neck Pain Naturally Without Drugs or Surgery! (Book)
by Dr. Richard F. Barrett $12.95
    Also available on audio cassette $12.95

Healed by Morning; Messages from God for the 21st Century on Herbs, Natural Healing & Drugs (Book)
by Dr. Richard F. Barrett $19.95
    Also available on audio cassette $19.95
    Purchase both books for only $27.95
    Purchase both audio cassettes for only $27.95

To Order: Call Pro-Solutions for Chiropractic at
1-877-942-4284
Prices do not include taxes, shipping and handling

Personal Financial Freedom

We have found that the number one obstacle to receiving health-care is that people falsely believe they do not have the financial resources to receive care. Therefore, many rely heavily on insurance coverage or do without. Professional entertainers, athletes and all financially sound individuals have the ability to choose any type of healthcare they desire. They are not bound by insurance limitations. They do what is right for themselves and their families without a question of cost. They understand the benefits of chiropractic and choose it to improve health and performance. You can afford chiropractic care. Health is a choice. Make it your priority. However, sometimes unexpected health issues or traumas arise creating a need for additional funds. Wouldn't it make sense to be prepared by having the financial resources available to care for yourself and your family? I think so too. Dr. Maurice Pisciottano has created a C.D. and booklet that will be useful in securing your financial goals and assuring you have the finances necessary for everything you need in life. It is called **Personal Financial Freedom**. Learn:

1) To reset your thinking so accumulation of money becomes easier than ever

2) Exactly how much money you will need to retire

3) How much weekly you need to set aside to achieve your financial goals for you and your family

Personal Financial Freedom
C.D. and Booklet $69.95

To Order: Call Pro-Solutions for Chiropractic at
1-877-942-4284
Prices do not include taxes, shipping and handling

Pro-Peak Performance

Would you like to know how to absolutely increase your energy level within 14 days? If you ever wondered if there was a simple yet effective way to safely increase your metabolism, boost your energy and improve body function, this is it!

Dr. Maurice Pisciottano has taught doctors around the country this valuable information. Many doctors routinely deliver this workshop program to their patients and the community. It has been responsible for changing the lives of countless individuals. We understand not everyone has access to these workshops. Therefore, Dr. Pisciottano has created a useful C.D. and booklet to walk you through this powerful information. This Pro-Peak Performance program is designed to share with you how to...

1) Increase your energy by up to 40% within 14 days

2) Prevent injuries by improving your attention

3) Eat correctly to achieve your ideal weight without dieting.

This is powerful information for everyone in the family, even the kids. If they are taught properly now, they should experience a healthier, happier, energy filled life.

Pro-Peak Performance
C.D. Program **$69.95**

Or purchase both programs
Pro-Peak Performance & Personal Financial Freedom
for **$119.90**

30 day money back guarantee if not completely satisfied

To Order: Call Pro-Solutions for Chiropractic at
1-877-942-4284
Prices do not include taxes, shipping and handling

Workshops, Lectures and Seminars

Dr. Pisciottano, Dr. Barrett, the contributing writers and the doctor from whom you may have received this book are available for lectures, seminars and workshops.

To reach **Dr. Maurice A. Pisciottano** call Pro-Solutions at 1-877-942-4284.

To reach **Dr. Richard F. Barrett** call 1-866-222-HEAL.

Ask your doctor about the following informative workshops and others to improve your health.

> **1) Peak Performance**
> **2) Trigger Point Therapy**

Find a Pro-Adjuster Doctor

To find a Pro-Adjuster Doctor in your area for a friend or family member that you are concerned about call:

**Pro-Solutions for Chiropractic at 1-877-942-4284
or on the web at www.pro-adjuster.com**